Love Yourself to Financial Abundance and Spiritual Joy:

How You Can Remove Blocks to Your Prosperity, Happiness and Inner Peace

Tom Marcoux

America's Communication Coach
Speaker-Author of 22 books
Blogger, BeHeardandBeTrusted.com

A QuickBreakthrough Publishing Edition

Copyright © 2013 Tom Marcoux Media, LLC
ISBN: 0615915760
ISBN-13: 978-0615915760

All rights reserved. No part of this book may be reproduced or transmitted in any form by any means electronic or mechanical, including photocopying, recording or by any information storage and retrieval system without written permission from the publisher.

QuickBreakthrough Publishing is an imprint of Tom Marcoux Media, LLC. More copies are available from the publisher, Tom Marcoux Media, LLC. Please call (415) 572-6609 or write TomSuperCoach@gmail.com

or visit www.TomSuperCoach.com

or Tom's blog: www.BeHeardandBeTrusted.com

This book was developed and written with care. Names and details were modified to respect privacy.

Guest articles are licensed by the contributors who own the copyright to their own work.

Disclaimer: The author and publisher acknowledge that each person's situation is unique, and that readers have full responsibility to seek consultations with health, financial, spiritual and legal professionals. The author and publisher make no representations or warranties of any kind, and the author and publisher shall not be liable for any special, consequential or exemplary damages resulting, in whole or in part, from the reader's use of, or reliance upon, this material.:

Other Books by Tom Marcoux:
- Be Heard and Be Trusted: How to Get What You Want
- Nothing Can Stop You This Year!
- Darkest Secrets of Persuasion and Seduction Masters
- Darkest Secrets of Charisma
- Darkest Secrets of Negotiation Masters
- Darkest Secrets of the Film and Television Industry Every Actor Should Know
- Darkest Secrets of Making a Pitch to the Film and Television Industry
- Darkest Secrets of Film Directing
- Darkest Secrets of Small Business Marketing

Praise for *Love Yourself to Financial Abundance and Spiritual Joy:*
"This powerful book can help you improve your financial situation. But it also reveals a deeper truth: if we take care of ourselves, that is, love ourselves enough to fulfill our mental, physical, emotional and spiritual needs, we will have the energy we need to handle financial storms." – Danek S. Kaus, author of *You Can Be Famous: Insider Secrets to Getting Free Publicity*

"Tom presents practical methods so you can expand your financial abundance. He goes a step further to helping you experience abundance in the moment. And he encourages you in ways to nurture yourself so you're ready for opportunities." – Linda L. Chappo, author of *Marry Yourself First: Your Key to Manifesting Loving Relationships*, marryyourselffirst.com

Praise for Tom Marcoux's Other Work

"*Create Your Best Life* is an uplifting and practical book. You'll learn skills in persuasion, charisma, confidence, influence and emotional strength — all vital elements to help you positively change the world. To make a dream come true, you'll need to get people enrolled in your vision. This is *the book* that helps you get great things done!" – Dr. JoAnn Dahlkoetter, author of *Your Performing Edge* and coach to CEOs and Olympic Gold Medalists

"In *Darkest Secrets of Persuasion and Seduction Masters*, learn useful countermeasures to protect you from being darkly manipulated."
– David Barron, co-author, *Power Persuasion*

"In *Be Heard and Be Trusted*, Tom's advice on how to remain true to yourself and establish authentic rapport with clients is both insightful and reality based. He [shows how] to establish oneself as a credible expert."
-Arthur P. Ciaramicoli, Ed.D., Ph.D., author *The Curse of the Capable*, and *The Power of Empathy*

"*Nothing Can Stop You This Year* is a treasure trove of tips, tools, and terrific ideas—practical, reassuring, and energizing! Tom provides wonderful resources for achieving your goals." – Elayne Savage, Ph.D., author of *Don't Take It Personally! The Art of Dealing with Rejection*

Visit Tom's blog: www.BeHeardandBeTrusted.com

Tom Marcoux

CONTENTS

Dedication and Acknowledgments	i
Book One: Love Yourself to Financial Abundance	7
Healing Your Relationship with Money by Noah St. John	84
The Fear of Trying by Elayne Savage, Ph.D.	87
Stellar Customer Service In Action by Rebecca Morgan, CSP	99
5 Fundamentals of Management Etiquette by Chip Conley	103
Create Success through Podcasts, Twitter by Danek S. Kaus	108
Book Two: Love Yourself to Spiritual Joy	115
Love's A Funny Thing by Allen Klein, MA, CSP	123
Book Three: Secrets of Being Unstoppable—Nonjudgment, Nonresistance and Nonattachment	143
Book Four. The Workbook: *What I Learned from Really Successful People—that has Made All the Difference*	197
A Final Word and Springboard to Your Dreams	219
Excerpt from *Be Heard and Be Trusted: How to Use Secrets from the Greatest Communicators to Get What You Want*	224
About the Author Tom Marcoux	234
Special Offer Just for Readers of this Book	236

DEDICATION AND ACKNOWLEDGEMENTS

This book is dedicated to the terrific book and film consultant, and author Johanna E. Mac Leod. It is also dedicated to the other team members. Thanks to Sherry Lusk and David MacDowell Blue for editing. Thanks to my father, Al Marcoux, for his concern and efforts for me. Thanks to my mother, Sumiyo Marcoux, a kind, generous soul. Thanks to Judita Bacinskaite for rendering this book's front cover. Thank you Johanna E. Mac Leod for rendering this book's back cover. Thanks to guest authors Chip Conley, C.J. Hayden, Danek S. Kaus, Allen Klein, Rebecca Morgan, Elaine Savage, Ph.D., and Noah St. John for their articles. Thank you to Shannon Seek for helping me to make my mark with my artwork/images in social media (SeekSolutions.com). Thank you to Higher Power. Thanks to our readers, audiences, clients, my graduate/college students and my team members of Tom Marcoux Media, LLC.

BOOK ONE:
LOVE YOURSELF TO
FINANCIAL ABUNDANCE

Need a way to improve your financial situation? Love yourself more.

Bear with me a moment. I never expected to write a book like this. Then five of my friends had their lives disrupted—each of them by money problems.

A question came to my mind: "If they loved themselves more, would they have been in better shape?"

Life can slam us with surprise disasters. Stock markets crash. Loans are called. Medical problems! It's reported 62.1% of all bankruptcies have a medical cause in the United States.

So what can we do?

First, we need to learn how to guard our personal energy and resources. To learn how to save money, live below our means and form both career and financial plans. We need to take daily steps.

What does that have to do with loving yourself? In essence, we're talking about taking good care of ourselves. If you had a friend visiting, you'd make sure he or she had a good meal and a comfortable place to sleep.

It's almost shocking how we don't give ourselves as much attention. And some of us even fail to do the basics of good nutrition, sleep, exercise, and spiritual health.

If you truly love yourself, you're better prepared.

Or if you do fall into a shocking, big financial mess, you'll have some reserve energy so that you can face the tough reality and make the hard decisions—and take the needed actions.

So why don't people take care of themselves? It's fear.

I've done that. I've let myself get too busy in just surviving and failed to do what's necessary to improve my life. But I've learned by personal experience that it's okay to feel the fear, and *it is still necessary* to develop some empowering emotions and take self-supportive action.

The idea is: when you love yourself, you do things for yourself as you would for a loved one.

I can relate to feeling tormented by money problems. I've been there. I'm not speaking from a life born of privilege. I was out of my parents' house at the age of 17. I lived in someone's basement. I spent a lot of time hungry while working two jobs and attending high school. My staples were spinach, broccoli, rice and canned tuna fish.

But I had a focus point: I am going to college. I was the first one in my family to earn a college degree.

When in college, I'd disappear when people in my dorm ordered pizza. Why? I didn't have money to participate in paying for it. So I didn't take a slice. I had no extra money for pizza; instead, I was paying for professional grade videotape so that I could make projects that would ultimately win awards including a special one at the Emmys.

But by letting my fears about money run my life, I missed out on times for nurturing college friendships and even networking.

With what I know *now*, I'd just make myself a peanut butter and jelly sandwich and sit and talk with the assembled college students. But back then, I was just too embarrassed. Lack of money was pushing me around.

Now, I ask you: Is lack of money pushing you around?
If so, this book can be helpful for your situation.

So I basically shut off opportunity—all because of embarrassment about my financial situation.

Later in life, I realized my mistake, and I saw I wasn't alone.

I was not treating myself as I would a friend.

I was on a path of formal education. But I blunted my opportunities because I was not treating myself with the kindness and support that I would show a beloved family member.

Aren't you like a family member to yourself? Or wouldn't it be better if you did show yourself kindness like you would to someone you love?

Further, I had **Three Realizations:**

When it comes to financial abundance, to love yourself includes times when you:

1) Take extra care of yourself because you need more energy to do extraordinary tasks.
2) Overcome resistance.
3) Take new action to get the support, training, and rehearsal time to develop new skills and new patterns of behavior.

1) Take extra care of yourself because you need more energy to do extraordinary tasks.

To increase our income we're going to need to do new things and sometimes put in extreme efforts. We need to take great care of ourselves because we need extra energy to do extraordinary things

To get rich, you can't be normal. — Noah St. John

Before we go further, let's get over one hurdle. Some people mistakenly think "love yourself" is "self-centered."
Stop!

Love yourself is kindness and support.
versus
Self-centered is misguided self-obsession, self-conceit, and one's ego running amuck.

To love yourself is to empower yourself to do good things in this world. If you give yourself good self-care (excellent nutrition, sleep and more), you have the power to express creativity and kindness. You even can demonstrate patience, calm and clarity of mind when other people need your help.

In my twenties, I learned the value of *staying strong and alert*. At the age of 21, I waited for a San Francisco bus at the corner of Mission and 22nd street. I noticed a small boy playing with his toy truck on the sidewalk near the curb. He was about six years old. No parent in sight.

The boy rolled his toy truck. It zoomed out of his hand, off the curb and into the street. The boy jumped to his feet, on his way to retrieve his toy.

My intuition barked at me to, *hold him*.

I grabbed him. At that moment, a bus smashed the toy

truck. Pieces flew about. The bus mangled the toy just as it would have the boy.

Later I told a friend. He asked how I felt, having saved this child. I felt different things. Gratitude. An intense feeling of pure gratitude that I did not hesitate. Curiously, I did not feel pride, but I did feel fear. A fear of what would have happened if I had hesitated.

Why might I have hesitated? Staying up too late for five nights would have left me alone in my own state of misery. If I had allowed my body to run down and I was ill, I might not have paid attention to the boy.

My point is: That morning I had enough sleep, so I was wide awake, able to listen to my intuition, and able to act quickly.

I invite you to realize that you need to take good care of yourself so that you can make good decisions. Sometimes a decision must be made quickly and you must take fast action.

Imagine what it would have been like if I hadn't acted. When I held the boy, he cried out in disappointment that the bus had demolished his toy. That was when his mother appeared and yelled at me in a language I didn't understand.

Her fury did not diminish the gratitude I felt that I had the resources to act quickly.

I recommend that you love yourself enough to take good care of yourself. Then you'll be ready and able to do what is needed and what improves life for all involved.

To take good care of yourself, consider moving *beyond* a "just getting by" approach to life. Make it a priority to get more rest, for example. With additional energy, you can focus on creating more and better in your life.

2) Overcome resistance.

When you love a child, you make sure she brushes her teeth. She'll likely give you resistance, but you'll brave it because the child's well-being is of primary importance. When you love yourself, you'll do the tough things to make sure that you become the person you want to be, the person who attracts success and financial abundance.

Here are two important details:

a) Kelly McGonigal, Ph.D., instructor of the acclaimed Stanford University course, "The Science of Willpower," notes that our ability to do the tough actions diminishes as the day goes on. Along this line, I focus on a practice, *Worst First*. I do the tough things as early in the day as possible.

b) Often, for some strange reason, *the task that can most benefit our lives is the one we resist*. It can be a form of self-sabotage. Why? Perhaps, we fear that our lives will change too much. The unknown can be daunting. And so I pay attention to what I'm resisting. This is another reason that I use the above method of Worst First.

3) Take new action to get the support, training, and rehearsal time to develop new skills and new patterns of behavior.

I started off as a shy 9-year-old boy terrified while playing the piano for seniors in a retirement home. So I gained the coaching and training—and did hours of rehearsal—to become a professional speaker and leader of companies. Why? Because I wanted to get big things done. I loved myself enough to invest in my training. I was also realistic in understanding that a lot of rehearsal would help develop new skills and new patterns of speaking and performing.

Now, I am your coach, through this book, so you can learn new methods and have support to develop new skills and patterns of behavior.

Recently, I posted a question to my 5,451 Facebook contacts—and I submit it to you now:

What positive thing would you do if you loved yourself enough or loved yourself more?

Let's go further.

When you love yourself, you know what makes you happy and your take action to support that.

Imagine that *you love yourself enough* to:

- do new things
- get the support you need
- get coaching
- fully commit to empowering habits and developing an Empowered Mindset

Step Forward into Financial Abundance

Abundance means "more than enough." In other words, you are functioning in a state of having reserves. Why? Life is constantly changing and flowing. And tough situations pop up. The car needs repair; dental work is required.

With reserves, you literally have financial abundance.

An important point is: It helps to develop emotional and spiritual reserves.

This is unusual in that many of us focus on "just getting by."

On the other hand, what does financial abundance take?

Let's dive in with **5 Principles for More Financial Abundance:**

    1) Do something that helps you earn money when you're not in the room.
    2) Target work that you do once and get paid again and again.
    3) Find something that is easy for you to do and hard for other people to do—that people will pay for.
    4) Overcome "feeling that you're not good enough"— and address the world showing your real expertise.
    5) Nurture yourself so you have an abundance of energy so you can jump at opportunities.

1. Do something that helps you earn money when you're not in the room.

For many of us, we only get paid when we're actually doing the labor.

For example, I have a friend who earns $400.00 per hour. That's still a limit.

On the other hand, I have other friends who earn money on Amazon.com and BarnesandNoble.com while they're sleeping. Their books and music are sold by Amazon, and the Amazon team's website does the actual in-the-moment sales work.

Look at your talents and skills. Can you convert something that you do into what might become scalable. "Scalable" refers to how you have something that can increase in scale. For example, someone who sells real estate could eventually have other real estate agents working for her.

C.J. Hayden (who has an article in this book) teaches people how to get more clients. She also licenses Get Clients

Now Facilitators. She notes, "Your first two clients will repay the cost of your license!"

Her program includes the following:

Eleven hours of facilitator training

Comprehensive Facilitator's Kit

Unlimited renewable teaching license

Ongoing support and community.

C.J.'s package (Facilitator training, Kit, and Teaching License) is $595.00. By the way, participants must renew their license each year for $99.00.

Additionally, C.J. states at her website: "Your facilitator's license requires that each person who participates in your programs must own a copy of the GET CLIENTS NOW! book." That's more book sales for C.J.

C.J. does *not* even teach the program. She has two people, "experienced business coaches personally selected by C.J.," provide the facilitator training.

C.J. can make only a limited amount of money by being in the room (or on the phone) and coaching one client at a time. Or the ceiling can be eliminated in that she can have numerous Facilitators all around the world. At this time, I see that her work is ongoing in 19 countries.

2. Target work that you do once and get paid again and again.

The above example about C.J. Hayden's licensed facilitators is about doing the work once and getting paid repeatedly. It all began with her book (now in its third edition).

Then she developed the materials for facilitator training. Then she trained two business coaches to teach the facilitator training.

Ideally, many of us will get to cut back on work hours as we get older. How? We need to find a "vehicle" that brings in cash flow. We often hear about real estate investing. Such activity brings its own risks. However, the model can work well in that a person buys appropriate property—let's say an apartment building—and then hires a manager.

Here is other work that is done once and then brings in continued revenue:

- write an ebook
- write a paperback book
- write a song
- sing a song, place a music video on YouTube, and make the song(s) available for purchase at iTunes.
- write a book, get someone else to record it, and place the book at Audible.com for sales.

I mentioned writing above and later in this book I have the section "How You Can Take the Suffering Out of Writing."

3. Find something that is easy for you to do and hard for other people to do—that people will pay for.

If you're good at something and you like it, you will likely devote extraordinary energy to do it better and better. The other essential elements are a) it's hard for others to do and b) people will pay you for it.

The final element is important. I may find writing poetry to be easy, but I do not know anyone who wants to pay for it. (I am currently writing a musical play. Perhaps, my songs will earn money at some point.)

Here's an example of the process, "easy for you/hard for others/people will pay." I recently talked with someone who was teaching improvisation skills to business people. "Jerry" has a degree in theater arts and acting and improvisation comes to him easily. But there are business people who find it hard to improvise in sales situations and business meetings. So now Jerry earns money in two ways: a) as a corporate speaker/trainer and b) as an acting instructor at a college.

4. Overcome "feeling that you're not good enough"— and address the world showing your real expertise.

Some years ago, I read a book by Bob Bly. He talked about how people deny that they have expertise.

Inspired by his words, I coined my own phrase: *"An expert is someone who has a system that people like and use."*

Why is this phrase helpful?

Because the phrase goes around the problem of "feeling not good enough," which is all about comparing oneself.

Instead, my phrase only points to three elements: a) a system, b) people like it, and c) they use it.

It does *not* fall into the comparison trap of "the expert must know more than anybody else on this topic."

Never compare your inside with somebody else's outside.
— Hugh Macleod

Many of us look at the successes of others and think they're much better than us at some job. The truth is that all successful people make mistakes just like anyone else does. We tend to only hear of their successes [or big mistakes if they crash.]

So focus on what you bring to the table.

When you are content to be simply yourself and don't compare or compete, everyone will respect you. — Lao Tzu

Ideally, you find out what unique value you bring and then you're not competing—you're creating your own category.

To begin this process, use *Empowering Questions*:

How am I enough? When did I do something valuable? Who did I help? How did I help?

When I talk about "overcome the feeling of not good enough," I'm often referring to NOT allowing the feeling to stop you.

You may still have feelings of doubt or even fear, but you move forward anyway.

For example, I may not be the best graphic novel writer—but I *am* a writer and I *have* a story to tell.

Plenty of works of art are imperfect.

Just move forward.

5. Nurture yourself so you have an abundance of energy so you can jump at opportunities.

When you truly love yourself, you take good care of yourself with appropriate nutrition, exercise, and sleep.

Another detail about having an abundance of energy: It's crucial to learn how to save money. Why? Many of us lose a lot of energy due to money worries.

Keep more money than you spend. I realize that this is not easy.

I can best illustrate this with a story about my father.

At one point, my father had a windfall of $1,600. A beverage truck had smashed his car, and he decided to take the money from the insurance company and live with a dented car.

He talked about taking a family vacation—my mom, me and him. At the time, I was quite busy teaching eight graduate school/college classes so I said, "How about you put the $1,600 into a Certificate of Deposit? It can be on a one month or even seven day plan."

My father did not put the money into CD (certificate of deposit). He spent the money on trinkets. We never went on that vacation.

My father did not practice the process of saving. Putting money aside in a CD was a foreign idea to him.

I've shared with my college students the idea of saving 10% of every check (even money that arrives as gifts).

The plan is to save enough to sustain you for a year without a job. That's the first step. After that, you may wish to look into forms of investments. You need to be careful though, because investing does carry risk.

My favorite form of investing is in my own skills development and in my own company.

Taking care of yourself well gives you an abundance of energy so you can jump at opportunities.

Here's top film director James Cameron's view of opportunities:

Doors don't just open for you. Every once in a while, one will open a crack. And you have to recognize that that's the moment. The door will open just a crack for a split-second, and you have to push it the rest of the way open. And you have to know that that's the moment to step through. It's a question of being prepared, knowing what you want, moving toward it. So that you are prepared in that moment to step through the door.

I always think that the universe is like a giant bank vault lock. You know, the tumblers are constantly moving. And every once in a while the tumblers line up and you've got to listen for the click.
— James Cameron

Some time before I heard Cameron's above comment, I wrote this:

When you answer the knock of opportunity, you need your bags already packed. — Tom Marcoux

For me, having your bags already packed means taking good care of yourself *plus training and coaching.* Additionally, you put in the effort with lots of rehearsal. Then you will be ready to answer the knock of opportunity.

Here is a practical example. Many people are now having an idea and then doing crowdfunding.

At Oxforddictionaries.com, *crowdfunding* is defined as "the practice of funding a project or venture by raising many small amounts of money from a large number of people, typically via the Internet."

I'm currently thinking about projects that may be suitable for crowdfunding so I interviewed a feature film director Mark Devendorf, who raised over $25,000 via Kickstarter.com. [In essence, Mark is serving as a coach for us on this topic.]

Interview with Mark Devendorf
(lightly edited)

Tom: Mark, you did something extraordinary: you made a feature film. And you did something else that's extraordinary: You *conducted a successful kickstarter.com [crowdfunding] campaign. What stands out for you about your kickstarter campaign?*

Mark: One thing: we shot and reshot the video interviews where we're [producers/directors] on camera—three times. We wrote out a script and then we did a first interview. We edited that and we realized that we were not saying things as quickly and as succinctly as we should.

We did it again, and we edited that down. We shot it one more time just to get the phrases. Because something that I've noticed with even the higher end kickstarter campaigns is that—someone will watch your video because they like vampires or certain authors but they'll tune out really quickly. Especially when you ask someone for money, [they feel like] you're wasting their time.

It took about three months to just do our kickstarter video. We just wanted to make it as tight, clear and succinct as we possibly could.

Tom: I saw your video and I was very impressed by it. It was terrific.

Mark: Thanks. I saw some videos by some great filmmakers from the 70's and 80's. [But] their pitches were just long and laborious. And I couldn't get through them even though the project was probably interesting.

Tom: Yes. You ARE filmmakers. So it stands that you could make a good promo film.

Mark: Yeah. And it's a fair amount of money [$25,000], so we definitely wanted to put some work into it. I did't think that it would be that much work. In order for the video to go viral, not just your family members have to be willing to sit through what you're saying. You have to get people to actually interested and engaged.

Tom: *I thought what really helped was your cross-cutting with actually footage that had filmed for your feature film. You guys were in a good situation in that you had already shot the film.*

Mark: Yes, we're almost there. It showed how close we were.

Tom: *How did you promote your kickstarter campaign? Because you were trying to reach beyond your immediate circle. How did you promote—?*

Mark: Our producer who is also my wife, Daria Matza, started a Twitter account a couple of months before and was trying to actively engage in people who were interested in the author Sheridan Le Fanu [author of the novel, *Carmilla*, —the source material for the feature film Mark co-directed]. I think we did a pretty short campaign, only about 30 days. Some people do 60 day campaigns. But every day, she was responding, putting out stuff, and reaching out to people. Someone would say, "I run this blog about this, can we interview you?"

We always responded. We'd be happy to talk to anyone who wanted to talk to us.

The most surprising thing was: from viewing other kickstarter campaigns, we thought that the majority of revenue [funds raised] would be from the low end pledges. Like people putting in $10.00. But we had 18 people who were not related to us at all—[that is,] 18 strangers put in $1,000.00.

Tom: Wow!

Mark: I think that's pretty unusual for kickstarter. Not completely unusual. The vast majority [of the funds] came from strangers. We were giving credits and titles and putting out packages. That's a testament about how strongly people, internationally (including Australia and other places) felt about the film and what we were showing.

Tom: *This is inspiring. It's inspiration for anyone who says, "I have an idea and I can get it done and pull people together." What is a mistake or something you can warn people about?*

Mark: In addition to having a laborious video to watch—if you're asking someone to give you money, you have to make it really clear what they're going to get. People can watch cat videos instantly—so you want everything to be clear and succinct. That's what we learned by editing our [video-pitch] over three months. The campaign is like a full-time job. It's not make a funny video and just collect dividends. [Instead,] you're working all the time on it.

The other thing is: we were putting up other videos and showing other links. We also launched our website and our Facebook page so people who wanted to see [things], they'd see the other stuff, too.

Tom: *Sounds good. One of my favorite questions to ask of people who accomplish big things is: Knowing what you know now, what would you have done differently?*

Mark: I would have probably done more work—more preparation and more work. It's hard to say. If we had failed the first time then I could answer that question better.

Tom: When you say "more work"—are you saying contact more blogs, knock on more doors?

Mark: Yeah. There were a few things we tried that were unsuccessful. We tried to get interviews in mainstream media. But most mainstream media wouldn't look at the film until it had a release date. They wanted to see a screener [a video of the finished film]. The smartest thing we could have done was hiring a press person—a publicist to keep pushing it. I feel like we could [gained more funds] above the level we reached.

Tom: Were you guys afraid while you were doing this campaign?

Mark: Oh, yeah! The first 10 days, we felt like there was no way we were going to make it. And we thought with so much time and energy, the thing was not going to pay off. There's no momentum; you've sent things out to people. It's only after the third time you send something that people start to look at it. So after the first 10 days, we thought, people are actually watching this.

A lot of my friends who have done this, they get their funding at the 11th hour. People put in $3,000.

[Instead,] we made it over [the required $25,000] two or three days before. And people kept putting in more money, and that was fantastic.

It takes a lot of energy to get that momentum going.

Tom: Here's a summary question. If your best friend wanted to do a kickstarter campaign, too—what would be the key you'd want *to tell them?*

Mark: Make it real clear what you're giving someone. Give it some value. A DVD is something you can hold in your hand. A credit or title is something that people can point to. Especially when you're unproven, you want to give them reassurance that you're actually going to finish this. [That it's] not just they will give money and it will go down some hole.

Keep refining your video and your message and clarify it. Have a video that is really exciting. One of the best kickstarter campaigns was for a beer cozy and the guy was just really dynamic. It was a really funny video and really entertaining. And the guy made a bunch of money. You had a really charismatic guy. He was good on camera.

People appreciate if you're speaking your own message. But make sure to practice your speech. You don't want to waste people's time.

Tom: Thanks so much for sharing these insights, Mark.

About *Styria*, the feature film which gained a successful Kickstarter.com campaign that raised $30,366 (with an original goal of $25,000):

In 1986, an alienated 16 year-old, Lara Hill (Eleanor Tomlinson), accompanies her art historian father (Stephen Rea) to an abandoned castle across the Iron Curtain. From a car crash outside of the castle, emerges the beautiful and enigmatic Carmilla (Julia Pietrucha). Lara secrets her away and the two are drawn into an intoxicating relationship. But when Carmilla mysteriously disappears, Lara's psychic wounds erupt into a living nightmare that consumes the entire town of Styria.

Written and Directed by:
Mauricio Chernovetzky & Mark Devendorf
Producer Daria Matza

MCMD Films
http://www.styriamovie.com/

* * *

Now, we're going to explore a number of topics that help you support your experience of financial abundance.

Topics:
1. How to Expand Your Financial Abundance
2. Attract Success: The Power of Your Personal Brand
3. How You Can Strength a Business or Personal Relationship
4. How to Enjoy Moment-to-Moment Abundance
5. Seize Your Greatest Advantage: Discover How to Connect With People So Well that the World Lies At Your Feet!
6. How to Take the Suffering Out of Writing
7. Love Yourself to Financial Abundance (The Cat Principles)
8. Lead Yourself and Lead Others
9. How You Can Get Whole-New Success
10. Love Yourself to Use Contracts Well
11. Some Unfiltered Truth about Love Yourself to Financial Abundance
12. Increase Your Energy and Banish Procrastination

13. How You Can Use a Top Success Technique—Listen Well

14. How You Can Instantly Feel Better and Get Things Done

* * * * * *

Topic #1
Book One: Love Yourself to Financial Abundance

How to Expand Your Financial Abundance

Would you like more money flowing your way? Have you ever thought about doing something with one of your creative ideas? We'll use the S.U.N. process:

S – solve your own problem
U – uncover boldness
N – nurture the idea

1. Solve your own problem

When you solve a problem that you have, you become an expert. How? You're directly experiencing what's wrong. You're highly motivated. You see what works, and that leads to you having true credibility.

For example, I went to a free seminar with two friends. As I sat there, I became angry about the manipulative techniques that I saw impacting my friends. That's when the idea for my book *Darkest Secrets of Persuasion and Seduction Masters: How to Protect Yourself and Turn the Power to Good* first arose.

I also thought of the times earlier in my life when

someone did something to try to take advantage of me. At those times, I could have used a book to help me protect myself. In the subsequent years, I trained and developed my own methods to stay strong in tough situations.

Further, I realized that I had often helped people protect themselves, teaching students how to swim and teaching karate to other individuals. So I could write an ebook and help even more people. The ebook consistently sells in the U.S., Canada, United Kingdom, Germany, France, and India. This inspired my team to also make it available as a paperback book.

Now, it's your turn. What problem have you solved for yourself? How could you turn that into a product that could help someone else? Or could you coach someone in skills to avoid or solve such problems?

2. Uncover boldness

When I first mentioned *Darkest Secrets of Persuasion and Seduction Masters*, my father was immediately against it. I also hesitated because some people might interpret the title as extreme.

But then I remembered a story about Walt Disney. When Walt Disney had the idea for Disneyland, everyone was against it, including his wife, his brother Roy (also his business partner) and the board of directors. Walt's wife, Lillian, wondered why Walt would like to make an amusement park. The ones she had seen had been covered in trash. Walt said, "My park will be clean!"

Walt was bold. He cashed in his life insurance policy for the funds to hire artists to do the first sketches of Disneyland.

Walt had to be bold because no one had ever seen a theme park before. The world needed Walt Disney to create the first such park.

Consider your own thoughts and feelings. Where could you act with boldness? Do you have an idea of a possible product or service?

Imagine doing an Internet search or reading a book or two on the subject. How could you take a small and appropriate risk and build on it?

3. Nurture the idea

When you first conceive of an idea, you may need to guard your energy. Why? Some people seem to be natural contrarians. Their reflex response is: "That won't work." Avoid them at the start!

At the beginning, your creative idea is in a fragile state. It can be killed by bringing in a contrarian too soon.

Also, at the start, you may be feeling ambivalent about the idea. So carefully pick someone you trust and then explore the idea.

- **Listen to yourself talk about the idea.**

Many people need to talk out their ideas in order to discover their own thoughts and feelings about their ideas. The same may be true for you. Plus, sometimes it's more important to discover your own impressions of the idea than hearing other people's opinions. Ultimately, your opinion is most important.

- **Notice your own feelings.**

Feelings can give you a glimpse of your intuitive impressions. Walt Disney had an intuition that Disneyland would be something new and wonderfully beneficial to many people. He had to trust his own feelings and intuition.

A person should set his goals as early as he can and devote all his energy and talent to getting there. With enough effort, he may achieve it. Or he may find something that is even more rewarding. But in the end, no matter what the outcome, he will know he has been alive. – Walt Disney

- **Further explore possibilities.**

To really create something that will result in financial abundance, think about a series.

For example, I've written nine *Darkest Secrets* books.

In addition to the one about Persuasion and Seduction Masters, here are the best selling ones:
- Darkest Secrets of Negotiation Masters
- Darkest Secrets of Charisma
- Darkest Secrets of Making a Pitch for the Television and Film Industry
- Darkest Secrets of Film Directing
- Darkest Secrets of the Film and Television Industry Every Actor Should Know

When I first began as a filmmaker, I was thinking about "one off" films—that is a good story but without the potential for sequels.

Now I focus on multiple series. I have three series of graphics novels (and eventual feature films)—and they're in different genres. Why? I do not know which of the series will be embraced by the marketplace at a certain time.

My series include: *TimePulse* (science fiction), *Jack AngelSword* (fantasy thriller), and *Crystal Pegasus* (children's fantasy).

* * *

A Special Note about Financial Abundance:

I mentioned "contrarians" above. Realize that some people have a real problem with talking about money or taking any action that involves a risk. You can feel their negative energy; they look down upon people who talk about doing projects that can create a big flow of financial abundance. So avoid talking to these contrarians about your projects and money.

Another important point is: money is an expression of energy. If you give great value, it's natural for people to want to hire you or purchase your projects.

I know several people who insist on talking about how someone lent them a car when they needed it, yet they do NOT want to talk about developing anything that can increase their financial well-being. That's okay for them.

But I do notice a number of people barely getting by. They talk about how the universe helped them pay one bill just in time. Wouldn't it be better to have financial abundance so that one can be calm and kind and share such financial abundance?

I have a friend who says, "I do not daydream" as if that were a badge of honor. On the other hand, I recall Steven Spielberg's comment: "I dream for a living." Spielberg imagined that he could pursue film making as a career, and he made his dream come true.

My point is: Consider making space for your own creativity. Open the door to the possibility that you can serve others by providing something of value.

Without a bit of hope, it's unlikely that one will take any action.

But this is *not* for you.

I invite you to solve a problem of your own and tune into a bit of hope—that is, just take a few moments to take a first look at helping others solve such a problem. On that path, you can find possibilities to serve others and increase financial abundance.

* * * * * *

Topic #2
Book One: Love Yourself to Financial Abundance

Attract Success: The Power of Your Personal Brand

Do you want more success at a faster rate? The process is centered around your personal brand. We'll use the Y.E.S. process:

Y – yield to how people categorize others
E – enlighten their perceptions of you
S – set up a progression of services

1. Yield to how people categorize others
What is a personal brand? On some level it is a category that people place one in. How does this work?

Here's an example. A new person, Nadia, joins your work team. When asked to describe Nadia, a number of people say things like: "She's nice" or "Nadia seems dedicated" or "She's a fast learner."

In this case, Nadia has a positive personal brand. In a few words it might be: "Dedicated, intelligent and good with people."

When I say, "yield to how people categorize others"—I mean just accept that this is how people respond to others. Do *not* waste time complaining about it. Just make sure that you take action to make your own personal brand positive.

On the other hand, I have a friend who has not been on time for any social event in seven years. I described this situation to my college students. I asked, "What do you think his personal brand is?" The college students in my public speaking class responded with these words: "disrespectful, unorganized, unreliable."

Now, I invite you to do things that create a positive personal brand. Here's a fast way to remember positive elements of a personal brand: Think **T.H.O.R.—trustworthy, helpful, organized and respectful.**

How do you give people a positive impression? Be a bit early for appointments, keep track of your agreements and address people with courtesy.

2. Enlighten their perceptions of you

To make good impressions, you need to be seen doing things well. In other words, skillfully shine light on your diligent efforts.

Some people like to keep their head down and "just do the work." That's not enough. Make sure that people can see how you're doing your job well.

One method is to provide a quick email message (if your supervisor is okay with email) in which you write something like this: "Just to keep you posted. Things are going well with Project XY. I'm two days ahead of schedule on _____."

Here are two benefits of this method. Not only does it keep your boss apprised of progress, but it also gently reminds her of the good work you are doing.

A warning: Do *not* go overboard with this method. Too

many of these types of emails would become annoying and could characterize the sender as an attention-seeker.

3. Set up a progression of services

Recently, one of my Facebook contacts asked a question: "Is it better to specialize in one thing or have a variety of services?"

I replied: "I've learned that the number of services depends on your personal brand. Your personal brand is your answer to "What are you best known for?"

If your target market sees you as the one and only best person for a particular service, then you might be able charge a lot for that one service. This is rare. For example, there is one best heart surgeon in the world—but only for a time, until the next person comes along.

Many people find it better to offer a "progression of services" that springs forth from their personal brand. The idea is that each service builds on the first one and provides more exclusive access to their areas of expertise.

First you start with a personal brand.

For example, I'm an expert coach helping and training people to communicate so well that they get what they want including success *and* fulfillment.

My services include the following: my blog, books, workshops, video training (entitled Top Five Group Elite Video Training System) and personal coaching.

You'll notice that potential clients can begin by reading a blog article and progress to having a personal coaching session with me:

Blog –> Book –> Workshop –> Personal Coaching (in the form of *Power Rehearsal for Crisis*)

My specialty is *Power Rehearsal for Crisis*.

There are many coaches, but there are none with my exact

background. With a degree in psychology, as a writer of 22 books (plus screenplays), and with training as both an actor and a feature film director, I can do something especially helpful: *Power Rehearsal for Crisis* (PRC).

During PRC, I can improvise and role-play so that my client can rehearse for the tough moments (or even crises) in life. I improvise dialogue so that the client is trained to respond to tough, spontaneous questions in a job interview or even harsh words when dealing with an upset family member. I even train some clients to be skilled at responding to tough questions posed by journalists.

My point is that you do better when you begin with an effective personal brand and then that brand informs what services you offer.

Your personal brand is your answer to "What are you best known for?"

Now, it's your turn. Take out a sheet of paper and write down your vivid answer to the "best known for" question.

Ultimately, your personal brand is a promise of performance. You assure the other person that you are trustworthy, competent and caring (about the project, team and customer).

Your best life begins with improving your skills of communication.

Show the world what you can do and how well you can do it.

Then success and fulfillment will blossom.

* * * * * *

Topic #3
Book One: Love Yourself to Financial Abundance

How You Can Strengthen a Business or Personal Relationship

Imagine that you can enrich your business and personal relationships. I've learned that being skillful in how we help one another is important. We'll use the N.O.W. process:

N - notice what support they REALLY want
O - open the dialogue on the positive
W - wonder if your ego wants to "help"

1. Notice what support they REALLY want
It begins with asking questions and really listening.

A friend had me view a rough cut of a video he intended to use for a kickstarter.com fundraising campaign.

As a feature film director, I had plenty of opinions of how I would to do the video differently. I restrained myself from gushing comments.

After viewing the film, I said, "Before I say anything, I'm wondering how I could be supportive of you at this time."

Immediately, my friend informed me that the video was due in two days. His tonality and word choice informed me: "I'm pretty much done with this. I do not really want feedback that says, 'Restructure the whole thing.'"

So flowing along with that, I asked, "What is the demographic of the people who you feel will fund your project?"

After I heard his reply, I said, "So how about adding ____ to the first 10 seconds because you told me the potential donors are interested in that?"

I had only offered something that related to what my friend said. In essence, I was supporting him "in *his* way."

My friend responded well; he was pleased that I was tuned into what was important to him. On the other hand, the interaction could have turned dark if I had merely "spilled all of my thoughts upon him."

As a comparative religion instructor to college students for over a decade, I'm familiar with a number of spiritual paths.

Here are some ideas that I have found useful for enhancing relationships.

When you are content to be simply yourself and don't compare or compete, everybody will respect you. - Lao Tzu

I am here only to be truly helpful. - A Course in Miracles

Out beyond ideas of wrongdoing and rightdoing, there is a field. I'll meet you there. - Rumi

Some scholars note that Rumi is identifying *ideas*—and not saying there is no right or no wrong.

We can also imagine that Rumi is inviting the reader *to drop reflexive judgment* of other people's ideas. This leads to the next method . . .

2. Open the dialogue on the positive

Before I offered any of my responses about my friend's rough cut video, I praised many things I found to be working well and what the evident intentions were in the structure of my friend's video.

By doing this, I created positive feelings. I also showed

that I'm really paying attention and appreciating my friend's hard work.

By starting with the positive, I created a comfortable atmosphere in which my friend was more open to suggestions and ideas.

3. Wonder if your ego wants to "help"

Over several years, I've noticed different times when someone close to me tried to be helpful. Sometimes, however, their efforts made me feel uncomfortable, and I wondered why.

Then I realized. The person did *not* hear me. They were slamming me with their opinions that exist in their own comfort zone.

(I've made this mistake, too.)

My thoughts returned to the quote: *"I am here only to be truly helpful."*

Then I realized an important distinction between different types of "help":

a) *"Lukewarm Helpful"*: Using my ego's comfort zone and talking about what I like and what I'm good at.
versus
b) *"Truly Helpful" or "Supportive"*: Looking to the person for clues as to how *she* wants to be supported by me.

Recently I helped a family member with her book. I had certain ideas and stylistic leanings. But I said sincerely, "I'm here to support you. You're the captain of this project." The book was finished in *her* voice.

In summary, I'm talking about being "truly helpful." If that is your purpose in the moment, you'll pause and notice how you're trying to help someone. Is it your ego making an instant judgment ("Oh! They're doing it all wrong!")?

Sometimes I've had to step back and realize that I can only help in ways that the other person *welcomes.* This has also meant that if someone is close to me, I've had to accept that I'll just feel uncomfortable if they tell me they do not want help. I'll be careful *not* to impose my ideas just to relieve my personal discomfort.

So let's take a moment and become aware if we're offering "Lukewarm Help" or "True Help."

Are we being *truly helpful?* Is that our purpose in the moment?

When you offer real support and it's accepted, blessings occur.

* * * * * *

Topic #4
Book One: Love Yourself to Financial Abundance

How to Enjoy Moment-to-Moment Abundance

Imagine that it's possible to feel that you're enjoying financial abundance even if you face significant bills. It's a matter of turning your focus to this present moment. We're not talking about living a life of naive denial. Instead, we're talking about exerting some mental discipline to turn your attention to the blessings that *are* present in this current moment. Now we'll cover the "3 C's" of enjoying Moment-to-Moment Abundance.

1. Come back to the present moment

I learned about this in Disneyland. Several years ago, I

was with a friend in Disneyland. She was unhappy. She didn't have enough money to buy every shirt and trinket that she desired. On the other hand, I was having a good time. I enjoyed just walking in the place. Here I was in a park with access to millions of dollars worth of entertainment and good atmosphere. I was enjoying the moment.

Sure I saw t-shirts and jackets and books I'd like to buy. I just let those thoughts flow by like leaves on a stream of water. And I paid attention to what positive things were in the present moment.

In the moment, I felt financial abundance. I was not time-traveling to worries about the future. Nor was I focusing on memories of regret.

I had enough. That's an important concept: having enough. And being in the present moment.

2. Care to give love and receive love

The more you love and also let yourself be loved, the more alive you feel. – Robert Holden

Love is the real work of your life. – Robert Holden

When you turn your thoughts to expressing love, you'll likely feel better. For one thing, you're not concentrating on what you're not getting. For example, one of my favorite memories was wrapping a present, years ago, for my then-girlfriend. As I sat below the Christmas tree, I felt great. I was fully immersed in the moment. I was not fretting that the gift was not expensive enough. I was just glad to express my love and appreciation.

3. Create prosperity consciousness

In each moment, we can perceive all that is potentially positive (prosperity consciousness) or all that may be negative (scarcity consciousness).

Before we go further, I'm *not* talking about a naive "just think positive thoughts" approach. I know life can be hard. I've endured some really tough times—there was violence slammed at me. Later, a close friend committed suicide.

In the face of those tough times, I've learned that it's important to strengthen oneself with an *Empowered Mindset*. And prosperity consciousness is part of that.

The opposite of prosperity consciousness is scarcity consciousness which is a default setting for many people. Why? It is pressed upon us as daily programming. For example, television commercials function in the pattern of "Feel bad. You don't have this product! If you had this product, then you'd feel happy." Scarcity consciousness is all about fear and "there's not enough!"

So it's better to develop an Empowered Mindset. It is something that I call *Opti-Realist Hope*.

For some people, *hope* is a distasteful word. In an earlier chapter, I mentioned a friend of mine who practically brags about not daydreaming. I'm sure he's trying to emphasize that he isn't wasting time with unreachable goals, but his declaration seems rather sad to me. A life without dreams is a life without hope, and we need hope. But we need a special kind of hope: *Opti-Realist Hope*.

When I talk about *Opti-Realist Hope*, I'm talking about a version of hope that relates to both optimism and realism. Numerous studies about optimism demonstrate that optimists have better health and more success. How? An optimist, especially a *realistic optimist*, will have the realistic hope that certain actions will yield positive outcomes. This person will take action. On the other hand, a person without hope will just sit there, claiming that taking action is a waste of effort.

Only with hope can we access the mental and emotional resources that lie within us. – Keith Harrell and Hattie Hill

When you love yourself, you will develop "Opti-Realist Hope."

To close this topic, I'll draw a distinction between two types of hope:

• **Opti-Realist Hope** – a version of hope that provides the energy to do the realistic, necessary actions of training and rehearsal to perform at your best and achieve your goals.
• **Wishing Hope** – a version of hope that holds to merely having positive thoughts or wishing without taking action.

Finally, prosperity consciousness is a courageous stance of facing life as it is and *still* pressing forward to make things better and better.

Truly, in each moment, you have a choice. You can let negative thoughts choke you like a bunch of weeds. Or you can take a courageous stance, **choose goals and with realism and optimism, and step toward making progress.**

* * * * * *

Topic #5
Book One: Love Yourself to Financial Abundance
Seize Your Greatest Advantage: Discover How to Connect With People So Well that the World Lies At Your Feet!

Just imagine everything you ever wanted is within your reach!

How? The world belongs to the great communicators. And you can learn what it takes to really reach people.

We'll use the E.A.T. process.

E - empower yourself
A - achieve in a step-up way
T - time your requests

1. Empower Yourself

And above all things, never think that you're not good enough yourself. A [person] should never think that. My belief is that in life people will take you at your own reckoning. - Isaac Asimov

Think of it! If you believe yourself capable and act that way, a significant number of people will follow your lead and find you capable.

For the most part, people are attracted to confidence. Make sure you walk and talk in a way that demonstrates that you know that you are competent.

To come across as confident, be careful of the stories you tell. Do NOT cut yourself down. Avoid comments like this: "I was stupid to have done ____."

I actually wrote a whole book about expressing

confidence and charisma entitled *Create Your Best Life: Unleash Your Charisma and Confidence to Change the World*. Here I want to share that each of us experiences life as an outpicturing of our own thoughts. If you think that you're worthy of good things and you put in the appropriate study, training and other efforts, you are likely to get good things in your life.

2. Achieve in a step-up way

YouTube.com has proven to be a great resource for many people. How? They demonstrate their talents and skills and then opportunities arrive for them.

For example, Justin Bieber recorded videos which Usher (the top singer, songwriter, producer) viewed on YouTube. Usher then signed Bieber to his company, and Bieber's career rose to great heights.

A number of speaker-authors (including me) post videos to YouTube.com to demonstrate how well we interact with audiences. These videos serve as 24/7 promotion films.

Another example: Fede Alvarez posted his short film *Panic Attack!* on YouTube.com in 2009. Sam Raimi (director of three *Spider-man* feature films) saw *Panic Attack!* and subsequently Alvarez was hired to direct the 2013 remake *Evil Dead* (budget: $17 million).

The point is: show the world what you can do on a small scale.

Then "step up" and keep expanding your efforts and your reach.

3. Time your requests

Pay close attention to the life and experiences of the person you wish to ask for something. If your employer is besieged by trouble, it is *not* a good time to ask for a salary increase.

On the other hand, if you're a freelancer and your client is happy with your work, it's a good time to ask for three or more referrals.

The same pattern works in personal relationships. Listen first to your loved one. Then the person is more likely to reciprocate and ask how you are doing.

I chose the acrostic E.A.T. in recognition that at certain times some of us "eat well" and other times some of us "eat scraps."

Let's do what is necessary to eat well. To do well in life, effective communication is key. Use the E.A.T. process to demonstrate to the world that you have talent, tact, skill and care.

People don't care how much you know until they know how much you care. — John C. Maxwell

The element of "Time your requests" does demonstrate a level of paying attention which many people find to be a prime example of caring.

* * * * * *

Topic #6
Book One: Love Yourself to Financial Abundance
How You Can Take the Suffering Out of Writing

At this moment, I have 22 books on Amazon.com. Many of them are in both paperback and Amazon Kindle forms.

Writing can expand your financial abundance. One thing that is great about this work is: You write the book *one time* and it keeps bringing in money, month after month.

Many people start writing a book but soon quit. Why? The way they go about writing a book creates needless suffering.

Instead, here are *7 Methods to Take Suffering Out of Writing*. The essence of this process is *teamwork*.

1. Save Time and Aggravation by Using the process of "__MORE__"

When I do not have the perfect word or sentence, I simply write "__MORE__" and continue writing my first draft. My father is the opposite. Each sentence must be perfect before he writes the next sentence. One of my friends said, "Tom, that's why you've written 22 books, and he's written none."

I'm able to write at a good pace because I know that I'll revisit the material in my next pass at the project.

2. Read the First Draft Aloud to Someone

My next step is to read my first draft aloud to someone. I revise the material as I read it to the person. Using this method, I find so many errors and opportunities to refine the material.

3. Talk it through with a Developmental Editor

I hire an editor who goes through the material and writes notes for me within the actual paragraphs. She places her comments in between "[ ]". On occasion, she includes a comment like: "It would be good if you'd address the situation of ..."

This helps me. Besides I find it interesting to have a *dialogue* with my editor on paper.

4. Revise after the Developmental Editor's Notes

As I handle each detail the Development Editor brings up, I know the material is getting better.

5. Have a Copyeditor Go Through the Material, and Then You Personally Revise the Material

My copyeditor goes through the material line by line to find any punctuation errors or missing words.

Then, I revise the material again. Sometimes, I put things back because I have my own style; other times I don't. But it's nice to have those options to choose from.

6. Submit the Work to a Proofreader

I submit the work to a proofreader. A writer friend of mine mentioned that she views her own manuscript one final time because sometimes her proofreader misses an error or two.

7. Realize that the book is a *snapshot of what you felt and thought at that particular moment.*

Writers can paralyze themselves if they're trying to write "the definitive book." I write freely because I realize that every book is really just a snapshot of what I thought and felt at a particular time. Ultimately, I'll let my whole body of work stand for my thoughts. By the way, I hope to think deeper as I progress through life. So if I do not agree with what I wrote ten years ago, I'm okay with that. Further, I can write a revised edition at some point; my book *Be Heard and Be Trusted* is currently in its Third Edition.

As I mentioned above, I can summarize my *no-suffering method of writing* with one word: teamwork. Sometimes, I have three editors working on different parts of one book simultaneously. I find that having such momentum keeps up my morale. I also have to keep up with submitting material to three people. So the project progresses at a good pace.

* * * * * *

Topic #7
(Book One: Love Yourself to Financial Abundance)
Love Yourself to Financial Abundance (The Cat Principles)

As I mentioned at the beginning of this book, I recently saw five of my friends have money troubles and I had a surprising question come to mind: "If they loved themselves more, would they have been in better shape?"

Then, my thoughts crystallized when I saw my cat walk into the room where I was typing on a desktop computer.

I realized that my cat naturally does three things that help him achieve the feline version of success: he is always himself, he is always where he needs to be, and he always asks for what he wants. You can do the same, and these can apply toward increasing your financial abundance.

1. Be yourself

My cat, Magic, simply expresses himself as a cat. He doesn't try to bark or chase cars.

Now, how does this apply to increasing our financial abundance? I'll give you an example. Some years ago, I sat in a room of 23 attorneys who did not want to be attorneys. They had the law degree but then discovered that they did not find the day-to-day work appealing. These were not happy, successful attorneys!

My point is that we are less likely to excel at what we do not like. And often what we do not like relates to where our skills and native abilities are lacking.

Instead, focus on your areas of great interest.

Secondly, don't compete—be yourself and create. To create more financial abundance it's often better to create your own category instead of trying to jump into a category that already has intense, existing competition.

For example, there is no one just like Whoopi Goldberg. She's an African American woman named after a cushion and a Jewish person. How's that?

Whoopi created her own stage name. Her original name was Caryn Elaine Johnson. This section is about "be yourself." And Whoopi expresses her own observations and viewpoint. Here's an example:

We're here for a reason. I believe a bit of the reason is to throw little torches out to lead people through the dark. - Whoopi Goldberg

2. Be where you can get what you want

I frequently encounter my cat in the kitchen. Why? That's where the food is. It's simple. He wants a treat, so he's right next to the refrigerator.

Now, it's your turn:

What do you want? And where is it?

For example, let's say you want to raise money for making a feature film. Where are the film investors? Some years ago, I attended a meeting in Palo Alto, California set up for film investors. If a filmmaker wanted to have a chance to get funded by these particular investors, she needed to be in that room at that time.

For some forms of business, you need to go where the fans are. Currently, there is a TV show entitled *Heroes of Cosplay*, which features people who travel to many comic book conventions. That's where the fans are.

3. Ask for what you want

I've just scratched under my cat's chin for the seventh time in a row. I'm not a cat owner; I am cat staff.

Magic speaks up and asks for what he wants: Attention and specifically to be scratched under his chin. When I scratch him behind the ears, he actually lifts his chin for me to scratch exactly where he wants.

How does this apply to increasing your financial abundance? In the following ways:

You need to . . .
- ask for the sale
- ask for someone to take a moment and listen to you
- ask for help
- ask for support
- ask for new ideas
- ask for referrals for your business

A Special Note about *Love Yourself* to Financial Abundance:

I'm emphasizing "love yourself" because, for many of us, to increase our income we're going to need to do new things and sometimes put in extreme efforts.

You may need to endure asking thirty people before you get the *yes* you're looking for. You may need to endure uncomfortable processes to get what you want. For example, some of my clients and graduate students feel shy and introverted at in-person networking events. With my coaching they learn how to make warm connections with new people. They need to rehearse and to fortify themselves before they walk into a networking event.

We need to take great care of ourselves because *we need extra energy to do extraordinary things.*

Make a plan.

And take action to expand your financial abundance.

In essence, love yourself to financial abundance.

* * * * * *

Topic #8
(Book One: Love Yourself to Financial Abundance)
Lead Yourself and Lead Others

As a leader of teams (feature films, graphic novels, books), I know that I have to "set a stage" in which team members can demonstrate their best skills and feel good about life and themselves. Leadership is a sacred trust. - Tom Marcoux

I'll say this in few words: When you *really want* more financial abundance, you will likely gather people to help you to do a project. Why? Because financial abundance flows in when you make something that provides big value. To make that happen, you often need a team. And a team calls for a real leader.

Here are three strategies of good leadership:

1. Cast the right team member for the task

Author Jim Collins wrote about how a leader is like a bus driver:

"If you have the right people on your bus, you don't need to worry about motivating them. The right people are self-motivated: Nothing beats being part of a team that is expected to produce great results. And . . . if you have the wrong people on the bus, nothing else matters."

In essence, Collins suggests that a leader gets the right people on the bus (on the team), the wrong people off the bus and the remaining right people in the right seats (in positions that are a good fit).

A number of filmmakers have observed that good casting is 80% of a film director's job.

Each leader needs to take great care in "casting" his or her team members. The right person for the right role.

For example, it took months of interviewing for me to find the person who proved to be an excellent match as the first illustrator for my graphic novel *Jack AngelSword*.

For me, it's a crucial process to work with a first illustrator. I tend to work with someone for 70 days in a row to make sure that the graphic novel's story is working.

I'm looking for someone to take my first ideas and make them come alive on the page. They bring their own creativity to the process and elaborate on my first ideas.

If I had settled for someone else earlier, the results might not have fulfilled my vision for the book.

2. Help them feel good about life and themselves. (Praising the team member's accountable actions.)

A prime responsibility of a good leader is to hold a vision for the project. You also hold a vision of what is excellent performance of yourself and each individual on the team. Make sure that you "catch people doing things right." Praise people. Give recognition for a job well done.

For example, one of my illustrators added an extra panel

to a graphic novel page. I praised her for her creativity. Soon she expanded one of my first sketches to three pages. This rough draft work remained in the final version of the graphic novel. Her creativity improved the entertainment value of the graphic novel. I was delighted.

Another part of being a good leader is to make sure that team members know that you care and that you're watching the whole process.

For example, when one of my interns was turning in work later that expected, I called him up and asked, "How are things going?" For interns, the idea is that school comes first. So I informed the intern that we can adjust the schedule if school or some difficulty in his family arises. He provided me with a list of dates that fit better so he could attend family events and still do well in school. He met those dates and provided some of the best work I've seen for my projects.

I hold team members (and myself) to be accountable. And I praise team members for meeting objectives that we've discussed. When a task is being assigned, we discuss the Estimated Completion Date (ECD) and I type that up in an email while we're talking. Then I send the email to both of us so we can be clear about the due dates.

3. Fulfill the leader's sacred trust.

As a leader you provide the vision. You are the example.

Currently, I am in the last three days of guiding my first illustrator of my graphic novel *Jack AngelSword*. If I do not provide her with a sketch of the next page of the graphic novel, she will not have work for the next day.

So each night *before* I go to sleep, I sketch a page of *Jack AngelSword* and send it via email to her (she's on the other side of the United States).

I can hold her accountable because I hold myself accountable to the team, too.

In conclusion, here are three of the responsibilities of a leader:
a) provide the vision
b) be the example of reliable behaviors
c) provide the structure, accountability—and "make it a game you can win."

When I talk about "make it a game you can win," I'm referring to two things. First, with accountability, a team member can succeed in completing work well and on time. Second, the team member feels good about herself because she is coming through for the team and herself.

For example, when I hire an intern, the person often needs good work for her portfolio. I make sure that we find projects that she will feel proud to have in her portfolio. By the end of a successful internship, she *wins* in a number of ways: a) she has good work for her portfolio, b) she has an excellent professional credit, c) she has gained personal coaching from me, and d) she has me to write letters of recommendation and return calls as her reference.

In essence, as a leader, I make it possible that each team member may win while being part of the project's effective completion.

Remember, a significant number of people increase their financial abundance by devoting time and energy as an excellent leader.

If your actions inspire others to dream more, learn more, do more and become more, you are a leader. - John Quincy Adams

I started leading at nine years old, making my first short film. My father (ex-Marine and former member of the Air Force) was my first cameraman.

Refining my leadership skills has been a priority for me in the ensuing decades.

I'll add one more attribute of a good leader: *healthy humility.* A good leader creates an atmosphere in which his or her perception can be augmented by helpful suggestions of trusted team members.

Lead well and everyone benefits.

* * * * * *

Topic #9
Book One: Love Yourself to Financial Abundance

How You Can Get Whole-New Success

Do you deeply hope for success you've never known? We'll use the N.O.W. process.

N - notice fear and still drop what's not working
O - organize how to stay okay even if something fails
W - wonder what new action you can take

1. Notice fear and still drop what's not working

Recently, I had to make a tough decision. About one month ago, I announced that I was going to give a "Create Your Best Life" workshop in September. Then something extraordinary happened. I finally found the right person to be the "first illustrator" for my graphic novel *Jack AngelSword*. This is like casting the lead actor of a feature film. Things work or they don't based on whether you have the correct key person.

So finding the right first illustrator is a big opportunity. Also, as a writer, I can get more done and do it better when I have momentum.

I realized that I needed more time for *Jack AngelSword*, but all of the activities associated with filling seats for a workshop would compete with that.

It was time to make an effective decision.

To have success you've never known, you need to stretch and "notice fear and still drop what's not working."

* Face fear.

I am truly reliable. If I say I'm going to do something, I do it. So if I change course in mid-stride in a project, it appears quite unlike me. It might even hurt my reputation. Fortunately, I had *not* set the date and had *not* collected any money for the proposed September workshop. Canceling the workshop at this point would not hurt anyone, myself included. So my fear of appearing inconsistent was actually a big deal only in my mind.

* Drop what's not working

Overscheduling my time does not work. Another way of saying this is "diluting my energy does not work." When I begin a graphic novel project, I like to do the first draft as one page a day for a continuous 70 days. This takes energy and creativity because for each of those days, I continuously rewrite the material and approach a blank page—before I apply my drawing pencil to paper.

Overscheduling dilutes energy and takes away your power to be calm, healthy and kind to people you encounter. It's best to drop overscheduling.

Now it's your turn. How can you improve your life by dropping something that is not working?

2. Organize how to stay okay even if something fails

Every project I do has a budget. Why? Some projects do not produce the income that my team prefers. Still, we need to have appropriate funds to keep the company going and keep the team members healthy and strong.

When you use a budget and organize how to stay okay even if something fails, you reduce fear. A lot!

For example, one of my clients produces a number of ebooks. She keeps the budget low for each book. Why? She does not know how many of the ebooks may fail to find a sizeable audience. Let's say she invests $400 for on ebook, but only sells ten at $4.99. This particular ebook "did not break even." She can be okay if two of her other ebooks together bring in $2,000. She made a profit of around $600.

Reducing fear guards your personal energy and keeps you healthy and strong.

3. Wonder what new action you can take

A couple of my friends spend too much time rehashing and wallowing in topics about things that were awful two days, a week or even years ago. What a waste of energy and time! It's better to reap wisdom and then make better decisions in the present.

To get new results, you need to do new things. It's that simple. I did not say that it's easy. I've noticed that people change for two reasons: desperation or inspiration (author Jim Rohn said as much).

I'll use either motivation. Why? Because I acknowledge that human beings often do get into action only to avoid pain. When that is the reality of the situation, then I can still use that insight as a springboard to action.

Now it's your turn.

Make a list of ten new actions you can take that will make

you a prime candidate for new success.

Go to the next step: identify how you can take action and have a plan so that you can still be okay even if something fails.

Now, with a better understanding and a little less fear, take some new, appropriate actions.

Show up and show the world how you have skills and talents to make a good contribution.

My company's mission is: *We create encouraging, energizing edutainment for our good and humankind's rise.*

This mission is in line with these ideas:

Nurture yourself and help others simultaneously.

Stay strong and you're more capable of compassionate and effective action.

Step forward and enjoy life.

* * * * * *

Topic #10
Book One: Love Yourself to Financial Abundance

Love Yourself to Use Contracts Well

I got pulled into two disputes. It began with my simple kind act of referring new clients to new vendors. My friends, the vendors, severely disappointed their new clients who were also friends of mine. All of sudden, I had four friends who were mad at each other. The problems could have been avoided if my two friends—the contractors—had used a contract!

Synchronistically, in the same week that these disputes were going on, I was called to teach contract writing in a college class. So I began my classroom discussion about contracts by talking about the *benefits* of contracts.

Here's where the "love yourself" approach comes in. Just like brushing your teeth, if you're going to take good care of yourself, you'll learn how to use a contract to protect yourself if you're a contractor or if you're a consumer hiring a contractor.

We'll look at the benefits as I spell them out using G.I.V.E.S. (as in what a contract *gives* you):

G – guard a friendship
I – inspire a customer to return
V – voice limits (no overworking; avoid constant revisions)
E – enjoy succeeding
S – set up that you're getting paid (half up front; pay as you go)

1. Guard a friendship

A good contract spells out people's expectations, and this helps you guard a friendship. When you put the details on paper, you can see what you both are agreeing to. You'll avoid promising too much. You'll also take time to identify if the client is thinking that some extras are part of the agreement. And in this situation, the contractor can put a realistic spin on the whole process.

2. Inspire a customer to return

Only happy and satisfied customers return. Without a contract and clear details about expectations and deliverables, both of my friends, the contractors gravely disappointed their new clients. Now these new clients will never return!

A good contract would have spelled out the tasks and deadlines. The contractor has a target and when he or she meets the target, the customer can see how the contractor did a good job and is reliable.

3. Voice limits (no overworking; avoid constant revisions)

Without a contract, a contractor may lock herself into overworking. How? Clients frequently change their minds. As the project goes along, they often get new ideas and sometimes want the contractor to scrap previous work. One problem may be that the client is demanding too many revisions of the work. Basically, with all of this extra work, the contractor may overwork and place her health or her other assignments with other clients in jeopardy.

It's better to have specifics in a contract like:

First Draft Due: June 5.
Client's Comments on First Draft Due: June 7.
First Revision Due: June 12.
Client's Comments for First Revision (if necessary)
Due: June 14
Final Revision and Final Version Due: June 21.

4. Enjoy succeeding

What is success for the project? Without specifics in a contract, both the contractor and the client may not have clear ideas as to what constitutes success for the completed project.

For example, a friend of mine writes press releases and then sends them out to 300 media contacts. It is hard to gauge the success of a publicity campaign because there are so many factors involved. The press release may be done well, but a disaster may become an "800 pound gorilla" that squeezes out other stories in the media. So a well-written press release may gain only a couple of media stories. This, of course, is bad news for the writer and his client.

So what can a P.R. consultant, like my friend, do? He can be clear that his work is to write a compelling press release and send it to the 300 media contacts. He canNOT guarantee the number of those media contacts that will run the story for his client.

5. Set up that you're getting paid (half up front; pay as you go)

Years ago, I worked for a small company that went out of business. I only lost $300 while other contractors lost thousands of dollars. Why? I specified that I was a pay-as-you-go contractor. It's important in your contract (if you're a contractor) that you're specific as to how and when you get paid.

A good practice is to require half of the fee up front before you begin work. Why? When you're working on this person's project, you must forego the opportunities offered by other potential clients. Also, if the client goes out of business, then this half-up front fee may the only compensation that you get for your work.

Here is an example:

For a six-week contract:
a) Half of the $2,000 fee up front.
b) At three weeks, the pay-as-you-go process begins.
Due Friday Week 4: $333.33
Due Friday Week 5: $333.33
Due Friday Week 6: $333.34

* * *

When you love yourself, you take good care of yourself. As a freelancer or contractor, you make sure that you use a good contract to protect yourself.

For many of us, studying about contracts is no fun.

However, losing money and precious energy and time is even worse.

So be kind to yourself.

Also, be good to your clients. How? By setting up a contract that makes it clear how you succeed in doing good work for them. When you do that, *your client feels better*. She or he does not feel taken advantage of. Your client does *not* feel neglected.

When you have a clear contract, you can truly enjoy succeeding.

* * * * * *

Topic #11
Book One: Love Yourself to Financial Abundance

Some Unfiltered Truth about Love Yourself to Financial Abundance

This brief section just poured out of me quickly. We're looking at answering some questions truthfully. I suggest that you write down your answers to these questions. Put them in a personal journal and do not show them to anyone (at least not yet).

If you feel the need, safely burn the piece of paper. The whole point is to tell the truth to yourself. This is not for others to read.

Ready for the questions?

Here goes:

1. Where are you hurting yourself?
2. Where are your habits hurting you and preventing you from keeping the money you earn?
3. What is your "Achilles' Heel" about money? Do you spend too much? Are you susceptible to something in particular? Shoes? (It's books for me.) DVDs? Blu-rays? Extravagant vacations?
4. How are you not living up to your potential?
5. What do you know is a good habit to form that would really help you?
6. Do you need a coach? Or therapist? Or counselor? To help you heal? To help you face your real situation and how you could toughen up and improve your life?

Now, here's the truth. **When you love yourself enough, you'll face the above questions and your personal answers—then you'll make a plan, set goals and take action.**

And start with small actions.

Use a principle I share often with clients and graduate students: **Better than Zero.** If you started walking 10 minutes a day, you'd become stronger. 10 minutes is Better than Zero.

Imagine studying five pages a day—material to expand your knowledge of your industry. You'd gain an advantage. Better than zero.

Love yourself enough to take action—even small actions—for Better than Zero.

* * * * * *

Topic #12
Book One: *Love Yourself to Financial Abundance*
Increase Your Energy and Banish Procrastination

Surround Yourself with the Compelling

Imagine that you can do what you previously thought impossible. How about making your impossible dreams come true?

When you surround yourself with the compelling, *you automatically go into action.* This is the road to banishing procrastination.

The Random House Dictionary defines to compel as "to force or drive, especially to a course of action ... to overpower ... to have a powerful and irresistible effect, influence." We want to overpower inertia, low moods, and procrastination. We want to consistently go into action to create the best for our life.

Anthony Robbins said, "It's not that life is boring, it's you that's boring ... You have impotent goals."

(Goals can be impotent because (1) they do not have one's

deepest desire as the first cause, or (2) the goal is actually someone else's goal—for example, saxophonist Kenny G's mother wanted him to get a college degree in something "practical." Research demonstrates that people lose resolve or interest in stretching themselves to pursue goals that do not arise from their personal core.)

With impotent goals, many people live a life of disappointment.

But you can have a better life than that! Join the people who create a fulfilling life. These achievers have found ways to make taking action a compelling part of life. They feel a pull to reach for more and better—and to learn how to make that happen.

Along these lines, I invite you to surround yourself with the compelling. Now, I'll share with you the 12 elements of the compelling.

The compelling includes 12 elements:
1. Your Milestones Binder
2. The inspiring work of the best in your industry
3. Your birthday celebration poster ("the doing now")
4. Books and audio programs that energize you
5. Memorized phrases
6. Project binder with a beckoning cover
7. Your easy, simple process to Keep Score and Achieve More.
8. Your process to Make It a Game You Can Win
9. Daily Journal of Victories and Blessings
10. Power of Alliances
11. Wall of Victory (or poster or corkboard)
12. Specific goal to brighten a loved one's life

12 Elements of the Compelling

1. Your Milestones Binder

Dr. Wayne Dyer said, "Some people live the same year ten times." They get stuck in a comfort zone. But a better life is available to you.

For example, my clients use a Milestones Binder to experience a new year every year. They use the Milestones Binder to celebrate what they do that is new and different in each year.

Their entries include achievements such as:
- Wrote my first press release and published an article in the newspaper for the first time
- Completed a draft of my novel for the first time
- Gave a talk at a Toastmasters meeting for the first time
- Sent a book proposal to an agent for the first time
- Tried tap dancing for the first time

Your benefits from using the Milestones Binder are two-fold.

First, you give yourself acknowledgement for your dedicated efforts.

We must celebrate our own small victories. We cannot wait for anyone to praise us—or even to care about our personal striving for a better life. You care, so you take notice—with your Milestones Binder.

You can give yourself a reward for each entry in your Milestones Binder.

Second, you gain incentive to stretch, grow, and try new activities. I find that I often anticipate writing my new accomplishment in the Milestones Binder—logging my efforts and giving myself credit. Then, I feel good again when I read the accomplishment to my romantic partner. I call that process the Moment of Appreciation. When she listens, I pause and say the accomplishment aloud, which helps me experience the good feelings of my personal stretching and growing.

2. The Inspiring Work of the Best in Your Industry

Who inspires you? What work gets you to say, "If I could only write (paint, make films or do something else) the way that person does!"

If you are an aspiring writer, keep copies of your favorite books near you. Look at the book covers. Glance at your favorite passages. Know in your heart that you can accomplish great things. Let your heroes in your industry light your path forward. For example, my client, Jack, wants to write a novel.

He has a copy of Stephen King's novel *The Gunslinger*, which includes the opening line:

The man in black fled across the desert, and the gunslinger followed.

Jack loves this line and it inspires him to continue his own novel writing.

You gain inspiration and energy by keeping your heroes' work at hand.

3. Your Birthday Celebration Poster ("The doing now")

Ever have a birthday and look around, saying to yourself, "This is nowhere close to how I expected my life to be at this age." It's happened to me. The good news is that the birthday celebration poster has saved me from energy-draining thoughts for many years! During the week prior to my 30th birthday, I was not happy about my life. I was nowhere near where I wanted to be. To rebel against depressive thoughts, I decided to take action and create a ritual to celebrate what I was doing.

Now, each year in the days prior to my birthday, I write up what I am currently doing and looking forward to in the coming 12 months. Then I gather my closest friends and we celebrate what I am currently doing (with the help of my team members). I place the 8 ½ x 11-inch "poster" on a stand and launch it the way one launches a ship. I use a tube with confetti instead of a bottle of champagne. The point is that I choose my thoughts. I choose to be grateful for the blessings that are in my life now. I have learned that the joy is in the doing, and I learned to keep up my morale with a birthday celebration poster.

4. Books & Audio Programs that Energize You

Many people who accomplish extraordinary feats in life have family members and friends with no such vision. How can you devote time with your people—those who have similar goals and who have gone through similar trials to achieve what they want? Through books and audio programs, you are acquainted with stories of people who have done or are doing what you want to do. This is like getting together with mentors. (It is also good to find mentors who you can meet in person.)

Hearing the stories of doers can help you counteract the counterproductive criticism of well-intentioned family members who may try to dissuade you from taking a calculated risk. These family members may want to help you avoid the pain of disappointment. But by not taking the calculated risk, one will still experience disappointment—often the worst kind of disappointment, "If only I had tried, it might have worked out well. But I'll never know. And I'll die here in this rut."

Over the years, my father has said, "I don't know anything about that." But I wanted to know about many things. So I went outside my father's circle and learned how to produce, write, and direct feature films. I learned how to work with attorneys to draw up fair and appropriate contracts. I learned how to form and lead companies.

Another example of moving beyond the small-scope thinking of loved ones is found in the experience of multimillionaire and author, Roger Dawson. As a young person in England, Roger talked about moving to America. His friends and family (31 people) advised him to avoid going to America. Later, Roger said, "I should have asked people who had already moved to America ... They would have said, 'It's great here [and there is] so much opportunity." Roger Dawson found fortune and fulfillment after he took action and moved to America.

Often the difference between a successful [person] and a failure is not one's better abilities or ideas, but the courage that one has to bet on his ideas, to take a calculated risk—and to act. - Maxwell Maltz

The calculated risk is the key. For example, if you are considering self-publishing a book, you can test the title by releasing a preliminary version as an e-book. Test the waters. That's using the power of a calculated risk.

Empowering books and audio programs offer the gift of inspiration and companionship. They enable you to make the best of your life.

5. Memorized Phrases

How can you instantly change the direction of your thoughts? With memorized phrases. When you have empowering ideas at instant recall, you can change the flow of your thinking.

Thoughts inspire feelings. If you want to feel better, think better. For years I have emphasized what I call *switch-phrases*. Imagine that your thoughts are on a train track. With an empowering switch-phrase, you can change the direction of your thoughts.

One can never consent to creep when one feels the impulse to soar. - Helen Keller

A quote can empower you. Having read Helen Keller's quote, you can ask these questions, "Am I creeping? What would soaring feel like to me? What do I need to do next to prepare to soar?"

And as I mentioned earlier, questions are the road to your intuition.

The answer is in the question. Ask better questions.

What am I learning here? How can we make this better? - Tom Marcoux

More quotes:

The superior [person] thinks always of virtue; the common man thinks of comfort. - Confucius

Let no one come to you without leaving better. - Mother Teresa

If you want others to be happy, practice compassion.
If you want to be happy, practice compassion.
- The Dalai Lama

Our fears must never hold us back from pursuing our hopes.
- President John F. Kennedy

I will not die an unlived life. I will not live in fear of falling or catching fire. I choose to inhabit my days, to allow my living to open me, to make me less afraid, more accessible; to loosen my heart until it becomes a wing, a torch, a promise. I choose to risk my significance, to live so that which came to me as seed goes to the next as blossom, and that which came to me as blossom, goes on as fruit.
- Dawna Markova

You can use a quote to transform your thinking and, eventually, your beliefs. Some people hold back from becoming successful because they have bought into their parents' biases that successful people are ruthless.

You can choose your personal definition of what a truly successful person does. Many of us find that "a ruthless but materially successful person" is not truly a success in our eyes.

Similarly, Helen, one of my clients, uses these quotes in her mind when her mother goes on a tirade "against rich people":

Success makes [people], for the most
part, humble, tolerant, and kind. Failure
makes people bitter and cruel.
- Somerset Maugham

I don't know what your destiny will be, but one thing I know: the only ones among you who will be really happy are those who will have sought and found how to serve. - Albert Schweitzer

The idea is that there are people who are successful *and* kind.

For example, author Richard Carlson was a kind, successful person that I knew before he passed away (when he was only 45).

Richard Carlson, author of the bestselling series *Don't Sweat the Small Stuff*, was kind to me. When we were both guests on a radio show, he took me aside and gave me some personal coaching. Now, that fits in with how I define success. Richard told me that *Don't Sweat the Small Stuff* was his tenth book. He loved to write (and I do, too), and he kept going through nine books previous to his extremely successful *Don't Sweat* series.

The knowledge of this kind of success helps people.

Through empowering quotes, you change your perception of what is possible. Yes, you can be successful and kind—and a spiritual person!

Choose your quotes and memorize them. You can empower yourself in seconds with a quote that moves your heart.

Would you like instant inspiration when you need it? Choose quotes of people you admire. For example, you can type a person's name into the search function of BrainyQuotes.com and often see his or her famous quotes. My clients have looked up Gandhi, Mother Teresa, Walt Disney, Martin Luther King, Jr., Steve Jobs, and others.

6. Project Binder with a Beckoning Cover

Do you have a project that has been at the back of your mind?

Have you wondered what you life would be like if you could just complete that novel or screenplay or some other project?

Here's the solution—set up a project binder. Place your project binder on your nightstand so you can see it upon awakening in the morning. The project binder can inspire you to write for 15 minutes or more in the morning.

That's how this book was finished. Every morning, I saw the beckoning project binder, and I wrote first thing in the morning. I printed out the pages and placed them in the binder.

Thus, every day I had a surge of good feelings as I saw and felt progress (pages)! The dream was coming true—step-by-step and page-by-page.

7. Keep Score and Achieve More

Professional writers keep track of how many words or pages they write each day. Bestselling author John Grisham said, "If you don't write one thousand words a day, then you are not serious about writing." Stephen King notes that he aims for 2,000 words a day.

These top authors are doing a process I call *Keep Score and Achieve More*. Many authors accomplish their writing goal and then go on to enjoy the rest of day—guilt-free!

The point is that making progress is fun. Keeping the daily word-count helps authors feel good and energized as they successfully make progress on a daily basis.

Keeping a log of steps accomplished can help in many situations:

- Business owner/salesperson: log of phone numbers dialed, voicemails left on answering machines and prospective customers reached voice-to-voice
- Married person: log of compliments or praise given to the spouse in one week
- Continuing education student: log of textbook pages read; log of hours devoted to completing a term paper

You gain the benefit of momentum and good feelings when you set up a process to Keep Score and Achieve More.

8. Make It a Game You Can Win

When you make a game you can win, you can feel good every day. For example, my process of logging my daily word-count helps me make writing into a game I can win.

Susan, one of my clients, was auditioning for feature films and commercials. I guided her to keep a journal of (1) what works and (2) areas to improve. When she writes an entry in her journal, she immediately congratulates herself for what she has done well (what works). Then she makes a note of something she may have left out (area to improve). The idea is to keep up morale and learn something from each activity. Regardless of how the audition has gone, Susan wins. Then, she closes her journal and is free to enjoy her next activity. You, too, can enjoy these good feelings.

I have worked with a number of clients who, before working with me, had lives in which they could not win. But that's not for you. You need to surround yourself with the compelling–positive items that charge you up emotionally to take action. So, be sure to use techniques that make taking action for your dreams into a game you can win–on a daily basis!

9. Daily Journal of Victories & Blessings

Ever lie down at bedtime and feel disappointed about how little you accomplished in a particular day? When I was in college, there were nights when I went to bed and felt terrible. I felt that I was losing, that I hadn't got enough done.

To counteract that feeling, I have written every night for years in my Daily Journal of Victories and Blessings. Now, I go to sleep feeling grateful and blessed. I give myself acknowledgements for my daily efforts.

Often, I exercise simply because I look forward to noting that victory in my Daily Journal of Victories and Blessings. This process works so well that I tend to exercise 360 days a year.

In my journal, I often write down that I have talked with friends and family members. Those moments on the phone are blessings in my life.

(Too many journals and binders for you?
Perhaps you feel that keeping Your Milestone Binder, Project binders, and Daily Journal of Victories and Blessings is too complicated. Here's the good news: this list of 12 Elements of the Compelling is really a menu. Choose any one method, use it consistently—and you win! Take action and keep going. And truly, nothing can stop you this year!)

10. Power of Alliances

When you really want to leap forward, create alliances.

Jack Canfield and Mark Victor Hansen's success soared to the stratosphere when they joined forces and created *Chicken Soup for the Soul*. Mark Victor Hansen says, "The power of 1

+ 1 equals eleven."

A mastermind group is valuable. Top Internet marketer and bestselling author Joe Vitale said, "A mastermind group can help you reach any goal ... A mastermind is a group, usually about six in number, and usually in non-competing businesses.

They meet to help each other achieve their goals ... On one level it's an obvious support group. Each person brings their own skill set, background business experience to the table, and everyone learns from another perspective. But from a Jungian perspective, you also create and tap into a larger mind, a type of third mind that is formed by a meeting of supportive people."

Joe Vitale continued, "The mastermind is run by whoever is the designated driver, so to speak. Basically, each person gets the chance to state their goals, their needs, and so forth ... Our group meets every Thursday, in person, at a restaurant. But I've been in two that were done entirely over the phone. And these days you could do them over the Internet with a webcam."

An interviewer said, "Being part of a mastermind group sounds like a shortcut to greater success. What if I can't find one?"

"You can start your own mastermind group," I replied.

When I started my own Breakthrough Mastermind Group, I used this form:

Breakthrough Mastermind Group Worksheet

Conference call on first & third Mondays each month, 9:00 – 9:30 p.m.

- 2 minutes for each person to present to the group their top goal and its corresponding obstacle.
- 5 minutes for person to receive feedback from group.

• 1 minute per person to state another goal to accomplish by the next session
• Any person can initiate a call after the meeting to another group member for follow-up.

Date:
Top Goal:
Obstacle:
Next Goal to Accomplish before Next Session:
Feedback:
Details that need follow-up with any due dates:

* * *

Delegate What You Hate and Overcome Procrastination
Researchers note that people often procrastinate due to the anticipation of pain. The following are powerful ideas:
• Delegate what you hate.
• If you delegate to yourself plus a friend, you have still delegated.

An interviewer asked, "What does that mean: 'delegate to music'?" I explained that if music puts you in a better mood or an energized mood, then you have "delegated" to your stronger self.

The idea of delegating to yourself plus a friend is an instance of the Power of Alliances. Some of my clients ask their romantic partner to help them get started on an onerous task for 15 minutes. Once the momentum is going, the partner can go on to some other activity.

Another tip: In my book, *10 Seconds to Wealth*, I describe the Morning 8. For 8 minutes in the morning, a number of my clients do an onerous task*: taxes paperwork or tedious clearing of clutter. But they are fresh and ready every morning to take action.

When you can overcome procrastination, truly nothing can stop you!

11. Wall of Victory

Mark Victor Hansen (coauthor of books in the *Chicken Soup for the Soul* series and creator of numerous products) has a Wall of Victory. He has photos that document hundreds of successful details of his life, including photos of himself with various notable people. These images lift his spirits.

Similarly, you can have a Wall of Victory, or at least a poster or corkboard of victory. Kim, one of my clients, has a Corkboard of Victory. She put a corkboard on the outside of her bathroom door. Currently, she has 3x5-inch cards showing parts of her screenplay in progress. She has also posted images of her favorite films, along with an image (crafted with Adobe Photoshop software) of herself sitting next to Oprah Winfrey.

She envisions becoming a major inspirational writer who is invited to be a guest on Oprah's TV show.

---

* Dr. Kevin P. Austin, director of the Student Counseling Services at California Institute of Technology notes, "People procrastinate because they experience emotions they don't want to feel when they attempt to do things.

Those emotions can be of helplessness, powerlessness, being overwhelmed, being controlled, sad, or resentful. The reasons a person has these feelings are not addressed by procrastinating, but the feelings themselves are avoided for awhile."

As part of her Corkboard of Victory, Kim has an image of herself receiving her diploma while shaking hands with the dean of the college she attended. She feels that she was able to complete college, so she can do just about anything.

You can energize yourself when you use a Wall of Victory.

12. Specific Goal to Brighten a Loved One's Life

Many of us just will not stretch to make our own life better.

We just don't seem to be wired that way. But give a mother the chance to enhance her daughter's life, and she will move heaven and earth.

Earlier in this book, I asked: "Are you a for-the-team person?"

Power flows when you set goals that enrich your life and your family's life. Also, some people like Oprah Winfrey set goals of giving to people who are suffering. If you have a cause (such as helping formerly battered women), you can add that to your goals.

Anthony Robbins decided that he needed to give from his financial abundance. His goal was to feed all the needy people in a particular area on Thanksgiving Day. To accomplish his goal, he needed to increase his financial abundance to the level of $4 million per year. Robbins felt the drive to take truly effective action to increase the profits of his business endeavors.

Remember, your great year (in which nothing can stop you) begins when you surround yourself with The Compelling.

Principle:
Surround Yourself with the Compelling.

Power Questions:
Which of the 12 Elements of the Compelling grabbed your attention? What can you do today to make that an empowering part of your life?

(For example, some of my clients use a Daily Journal of Victories and Blessings.)

* * * * * *

Topic #13
Book One: *Love Yourself to Financial Abundance*
How You Can Use a Top Success Technique—Listen Well

Do you want to get people to like you and trust you quickly? Learn to listen well. Here are three methods:

A – attend
R – reflect
E – engage emotions

1. Attend
Give your full attention. Make sure that your heart faces their heart ("Heart faces heart.")

At times, I begin a conversation with, "I'm listening. What would you like me to know about the situation?" The reason for this beginning is sometimes the situation may have some heat to it. When I listen first, the tension drains from the situation.

Think about it: How often does one get fully listened to? Can you imagine what a relief it is to have your thoughts and feelings heard without interruption or automatic judgment?

Near the end of a conversation, I ask, "Is there anything else you need me to know?" Again, this is about giving full attention.

2. Reflect

Provide what I call "Reflective Replies." Reflect their concerns and emotions. Say things like: "That sounds frustrating" or "That sounds hard to endure."

Why is this valuable?

First, we often do not know if someone understands the meaning behind our words. Reflective Replies assure the speaker that you understand the meaning. Or if you say something a bit off, the speaker can use other words to clarify his or her meaning.

Second, you do NOT tell another person what they are feeling. You provide a gentle phrase: "That sounds . . ."

For example, you might say, "That sounds frustrating." But the person says, "Not frustrating, disappointing."

Then you can ask, "What disappointed you the most about this situation?" That question signals that you are being fully present with the person in the moment.

3. Engage emotions

Help the person feel it is safe to share his or her feelings. Someone may say, "That driver made me mad." Often, I'll reply, "Okay." For me "okay" is neutral. I do not have to agree. By saying "okay" I'm communicating, "I'm hearing you. It's okay to feel whatever you're feeling."

I have an elderly relative who has horrible habits when it

comes to listening. This guy only pauses between things he wants to say. It does NOT feel safe to express a feeling around him. I have actually said to him, "You cannot logic me out of my feelings. I get to feel the way I feel about this."

Instead, as a good listener, you make a safe place for the other person to express his or her feelings. Once a person feels heard, often the energy about a situation "cools off."

Listening well is a big part of creating success and fulfillment in our lives.

How do you get loyalty and reliable efforts from other people? Listen to them well.

Start practicing today.

You'll discover how your business and personal relationships improve.

* * * * * *

Topic #14:
(Book One: Love Yourself to Financial Abundance)

How You Can Instantly Feel Better and Get Things Done

Do you want to shake off the pain of disappointment and approach life with more energy? To create financial abundance, you need to reduce time lost to disempowering emotions. You'll find that you need lots of personal energy to do things you've never done before. You can use the power of "act as if." Here's the A.S. process:

A – act
S – support yourself with a "30-30-30 Shield"

1. Act
Actions can inspire our feelings.

It is easier to act yourself into a new way of feeling than to feel yourself into a new way of acting. – Harry Stack Sullivan

If someone says something that offends you, consider taking a walk. Get the stress out of your body by moving.

Here's an important action: sit up straight. Why? Allowing ourselves to slouch creates trouble. We can actually lower our mood by adopting a "defeated posture." To shake free of that, cultivate good posture. You can breathe easier.

I learned about good posture when three physical therapists helped me recover from injuries I sustained in a car accident. They assured me that sitting with one's vertebra aligned takes less energy. The back was designed for the bones to line up and provide a resting posture. Slouching in a chair requires some muscles to stay active and hold you up.

Discover how taking action (sitting up or moving), can improve your mood.

2. Support yourself with a "30-30-30 Shield."
When asked how she deals with a lot of pressure (as a pro athlete, a *Sports Illustrated* model, a mother and the wife of celebrity surfer Laird Hamilton), Gabrielle Reese said, **"In life, you will always have 30 percent of the people who love you, 30 percent who hate you, and 30 percent who couldn't care less."**

We can use the above quote as part of what I call a "30-30-30 Shield." How?

The ideas of Gabrielle's quote release us from trying to be perfect and from trying to please everyone.

Many of us experience a huge drop in energy and motivation when under-fire by others' criticism.

Your first thoughts might be on the order of: "Oh, no! I can't do anything right. Nobody's going to like [my book, my blog, my artwork, etc.]."

Instead, invoke your 30-30-30 Shield.

You can assess: "Is this person part of the 30 percent who will never understand the value of what I'm doing? Is he someone who will never care? If so, I can dismiss him from my mind."

With the above, you could even "shield" your self-esteem. When someone slams criticism at us, it can feel like a blow to our self-esteem.

But with the 30-30-30 Shield we can assess: "This person just doesn't care about what I care about." or "Evidently, I made artwork that does not appeal to this person. I'll serve my own audience."

We can devote more time to thinking about the 30% who do love us:

Being deeply loved by someone gives you strength, while loving someone deeply gives you courage. – Lao Tzu.

In summary, you can change your feelings with two processes. First, take action to release stress.

Secondly, guide your own thoughts. Don't let them fall into a negative spiral. Instead, employ your 30-30-30 Shield and rejoice in being fully alive. Experiment with creativity, take appropriate risks, and concentrate on those people who can relate to your style of creativity.

* * * * * *

Many of us need to heal our relationship with money. Now, Noah St. John shares some valuable ideas.

Healing Your Relationship with Money
by Noah St. John

Many people have a very unhealthy relationship with money.

In *The Book of Afformations®*, I share some simple but powerful ideas:

1. Desire is the first seed of mind.
2. You have to believe you can be, do, or have what you want.
3. Lack of belief is the biggest thing stopping most people from making a lot more money.
4. You usually have to do something uncomfortable to get the thing you really want.
5. Stop waiting for things to change. Instead, make the changes you want to see in your life.

In order to get the things you want in life, you often have to do things that feel uncomfortable…

Exactly!

Your actions will tend to be tentative, fearful, and anticipating failure…

And your results will tend to be less than desirable.

On the other hand, what if you grew up experiencing an abundance of love, support, and opportunity?

What then would your assumptions about life be?

Probably things like...

I can live the life I choose
There's plenty of opportunity out there!
I can have the things I want

The problem is, of course, that most of us did NOT grow up experiencing an abundance of love, support, or opportunity...

In fact, the vast majority of human beings grow up in an environment of *not enough*...

Not enough love
Not enough support
Not enough money
Not enough opportunity

That's why the vast majority of human beings have formed negative, disempowering assumptions about their lives...

And why their actions and results naturally follow.

However, let me give you some wonderful news...

No matter what happened in the past, no one can force you to think certain thoughts.

YOU, and you alone, control your thoughts, beliefs, and actions.

That's why the point of using Afformations is NOT to find all the answers...

The point is to form new beliefs that you CAN be, do, and have the things you want...

And let your mind find a way to make it so.

Take Action Step:
Replace your disempowering assumptions with Aformations — and watch the miracles happen in your life, too…

About Noah St. John
Noah St. John is the author of *The Book of Afformations®: Discovering The Missing Piece to Abundant Health, Wealth, Love, and Happiness* (Hay House). He is famous for inventing Afformations® and creating high-impact, customized strategies for fast-growing companies and leading organizations around the world. His sought-after advice is known as the "secret sauce" for creating instant superstar performance in high-growth businesses.

Noah's engaging and down-to-earth speaking style always gets high marks from audiences. As the leading authority on how to eliminate limiting beliefs, Noah delivers speeches, seminars, and mastermind programs that have been called "mandatory for anyone who wants to succeed in business."

He also appears frequently in the news worldwide, including CNN, ABC, NBC, CBS, Fox, National Public Radio, Parade, *Woman's Day, Los Angeles Business Journal, The Washington Post, Chicago Sun-Times, Selling Power, Forbes.com,* and *The Huffington Post.*

Founder of the international coaching and training corporation SuccessClinic.com, Noah is known for producing innovative products and programs that have helped to improve tens of thousands of lives and businesses around the world.

Fun fact: Noah once won an all-expenses-paid trip to Hawaii on the game show *Concentration,* where he missed winning a new car by three seconds. (Note: He had not yet discovered Afformations.)

Get the first chapter of *The Book of Afformations* FREE at www.NoahStJohn.com

* * * * * *

For many of us, a way to more financial abundance is to start a business. Even if you love the basic parts of your business, you might find yourself in over your head. It's important to start a business that has a viable business model. Now, C.J. Hayden will share insights about that process.

Entrepreneur on a Mission: What's Your Business Model?
by C.J. Hayden

If you spend any amount of time hanging around with entrepreneurial innovators, visionaries, and reformers, you'll hear this question frequently. Entrepreneur #1 sketches out his or her brave new idea for making a living while changing the world, and Entrepreneur #2 asks, "What's your business model?"

It's an important question to be able to answer. Simply put, your business model is how you intend to generate sufficient revenue to meet expenses and earn a profit. If a mission-driven enterprise is going to be sustainable, it needs to have clearly defined income streams that will be sufficient to fuel your mission, cover your expenses, support you and your family, and provide for the future. That can be a tall order.

Unfortunately, many entrepreneurs on a mission don't actually have a profit-making plan. And some of those who think they have one are relying more on guesswork than they are on analysis.

There are a wide variety of established business models available. Most service professionals use the billable hours model and request payment for each hour they work. When your enterprise includes not just service, but products, programs, and processes, you expand the possibilities for the type of model, or combination of models, you can use.

Here are some examples of business models used by many of my clients that you can draw from:

Fee for Service Models

Day Rate — Instead of charging by the hour, you can charge by the day or half-day. This imposes a minimum on your clients, avoiding short appointments that fragment your work schedule. Examples:

- Environmental market researcher conducting focus groups
- Massage therapist providing on-site massage for organizations

Project Fee — Charging a flat fee for each project allows you to bill for time you spend planning, researching, or just thinking about your client's issues. Clients often prefer flat fees because they can budget their funds more accurately. Examples:

- Sustainability consulting firm advising clients on implementing responsible practices
- Psychologist offering psychological testing and assessment

Monthly Retainer — When you ask clients to pay by the month in advance, you can charge for your availability, not just service delivered. Your retainer can guarantee you a fixed number of hours. If the client uses less, you still get paid. If they use more, you can charge extra. Examples:

- Recovery coach offering as-needed calls and e-mails in between sessions
- Political consultant providing ongoing campaign management and advice

Subcontractors/Employees — You can hire or contract with other professionals and have them deliver services on behalf of your company. These may be people who come to you with appropriate skills and experience already, or people you train to use your approach. Clients pay your company for these services and you keep a percentage for yourself. Examples:

- Learning center with multiple teachers on staff
- Diversity training firm with trainers in multiple locations

Product- or Process-Based Models

Flat Fee — A wide variety of items can be sold for a flat fee to increase revenue for your enterprise. "Products" can also include services delivered in a defined package. Your buyers may be either existing clients, or others who can't afford to hire you individually. Examples:

- Cause marketing consultant packaging her wisdom in a do-it-yourself kit

- Mediator offering public conflict resolution seminars

Subscription/Membership — Providing products or services by subscription, or memberships in your community, can provide a steady source of income and reduce marketing time. A sale made only once can continue to provide revenue. Examples:

- Youth leadership trainer selling an educational CD series by monthly subscription
- Nurse consultant hosting an online community for people with chronic illness

Back-End Sales — Also called the "bait and hook" or "razor and blades" model, where you sell a product or service that requires periodic updates at an additional cost. Examples:

- Vegan weight loss expert offering frozen packaged meals delivered monthly
- Database of sustainable ingredients for cosmetics requiring quarterly updates

Licensing/Franchising — Packaging your approach so that others can replicate it with their own clients or in different locations. Your licensees or franchisees pay you a start-up fee to acquire your package, which may also include training. You may also offer them ongoing training and support in return for an annual renewal fee or a percentage of their earnings. Examples:

- Social enterprise employing homeless workers offers their model to other cities
- Trauma recovery therapist certifies other therapists in his/her approach

Any one of these models can be used to build an entire business, or you can combine different models together. For example, a consultant could charge a flat fee for assessments, then a day rate to deliver services. A coach could charge a subscription fee for group clients and a monthly retainer for clients worked with individually.

As you can see, a sustainable business model can make it possible for your brilliant ideas for changing the world to also provide you with a good living.

Here are some coaching questions to ask yourself to design a better business model:

- How far do you want your mission to reach? Will you be satisfied with the number of clients you can serve yourself, or will you need to expand in order to make the impact you seek?
- How much do you want or need to earn in order to further your mission, cover your business expenses, support you and your family, and provide for your future and that of your enterprise? Is it realistic to expect that level of earnings with your current business model?
- What's your vision of how you most like to spend your time? Serving clients? Creating new work? Working alone? Participating on a team? Learning and experimenting? Organizing and planning? Hanging out online? Speaking or teaching? Traveling? Hosting others in a place of your own?
- When you read the examples of business models above, which ones sparked your interest? Can you see yourself in any of these models? Which seemed

to speak most to your skills, talents, and preferred work style?

Don't let your passion for world-changing and all your hard work go to waste. Begin today to develop a business model that can sustain both you and your mission.

— —

C.J. Hayden, MCC, CPCC, is the bestselling author of *Get Clients Now!*, *The One-Person Marketing Plan Workbook*, *50 Ways Coaches Can Change the World*, and over 400 articles. C.J. is a business coach and teacher who helps entrepreneurs get clients, get strategic, and get things done. Her company, Wings for Business, specializes in serving independent professionals and solopreneurs.

A popular speaker and workshop leader, C.J. has presented hundreds of programs on marketing and entrepreneurship to corporate clients, professional associations, and small businesses. She has taught marketing for John F. Kennedy University, Mills College, the U.S. Small Business Administration, and SCORE. She contributes regularly to dozens of magazines and websites, including *Home Business*, *RainToday*, *Salesopedia*, and *About.com*.

Visit C.J. at www.cjhayden.com

* * * * * *

No conversation about love yourself is complete without discussing *love yourself enough to become skillful about handling fear.*

Along this line, I now share with you an article by Dr. Elayne Savage.

The Fear of Trying
By Elayne Savage, Ph.D.

By its nature putting oneself 'out there' involves the possibility of rejection. And rejection hurts.

When I'm about to begin a new creative project, something holds me back. It's especially challenging when writing is involved. What a struggle it was to put out the first edition of my e-letter, 'Tips from The Queen of Rejection.'

Each time I challenge myself, I learn fascinating things about my relationship to Fear.

Tripping Over My Own Stumbling Blocks

I drag my feet. Every diversion that comes along sidetracks me. I even find myself sorting through stacks of papers and cleaning out file cabinets.

I'm tripping over my own stumbling blocks.

Why is starting a new project so difficult? Something is interfering, displacing anticipation, and eclipsing hope. Then I recognize the intruder.

It is Fear.

The Fear Team Roars In

The Fear Team comes roaring onto the field led by The Fear of

Rejection and its evil twin, the Fear of Failure. They're joined by the Fear of Success and the Fear of Being Visible.

Warming up on the sidelines are the Fear of Disappointment and the Fear of Judgment and Criticism.

Make no mistake about it, however. Fear of Rejection is the team leader, the foundation for all the other Fears.

I hear voices in the background and stop to listen. The Fear Team brought along a rooting section. Well, that's OK. I can muster up my own pep squad.

Both sides try to out-shout each other: "You can't do it! You can't do it!" answered by "Yes, I can! Yes, I can!"

"I have lots to say on this subject!" "You have nothing to say!" "Lots!" "Nothing!" "Lots!" "Nothing!"

Opposing voices swirl around in my head. Conflicting emotion skirmish with one another.

The confusion makes me stressed and anxious. I become immobilized.

The Queen Calls a Time Out.

It's time to sort things out. It's too hard to see options through this haze of confusion. When we're unable to make choices, we feel stuck. And when we're so immobilized, making choices becomes even more difficult.

This exhausting tug-of-war between the voices is ambivalence. It involves the presence of simultaneously conflicting thoughts, ideas or feelings.

Those Whispers and Roars of Ambivalence

For some folks the word 'ambivalence' means 'love and hate' or 'good and bad.' But there are many kinds of ambivalent feelings and thoughts.

When your internal voices start skirmishing with one another, this conflict leads to uncertainty and confusion.

The confusion creates anxiety. The anxiety causes freezing

up, becoming immobilized. This degree of ambivalence surely isn't productive.

It takes a lot of energy to deal with these competing voices. Wouldn't you rather put your energy into something more creative?

By moving past the ambivalence, you'll be opening space for making choices.

5 Tips for Taming Ambivalence

1 - Honor both voices by giving them a chance to be heard. When you only listen to one voice you are rejecting the other.

2 - Name That Fear. Can you name the Fear that is immobilizing you? This allows you to see it differently and recognize possible options.

3 - Learn more about the Fear by asking yourself:

If I put myself "out there" it would mean _____.

If I fail, it would mean _____.

If I succeed, it would mean _____.

If I feel too visible what might happen? _____.

4 - Approach the Fear with some detachment. I call it 'walking alongside yourself.' Step back enough to recognize when you are starting down that old path of doubt and fear.

5 - Then, ask yourself, "Do I want to continue down this path? I could retrace my steps and make the choice to go down a different road."

Messages from Many People

Ambivalence is often influenced by the messages we hear in our early years. And I was running smack into a wall of these childhood messages:

"You're such a dreamer."
"What makes you think you can do that?"
"Who are you?"
"Who are you?"
"Who are you?"

You, too, may have memories of admonitions received from parents, teachers, or peers. In the last twenty-five years, I've heard hundreds of poignant stories from my counseling and consulting clients.

To complicate things even more, these warnings can be unspoken family messages passed down from generation to generation.

Warnings like these are rejecting messages. They discount, dismiss and diminish. Over time we interpret these warnings as "Be careful." Caution like this isn't conducive to exploring new directions or writing first issues of newsletters.

Trying to sort it all out, I ask myself an important question:

"What am I afraid of?"

- Could I be comparing my proposed project to others out there?

Sure.

- Might this involve making the commitment necessary to produce something regularly?

Absolutely.

- Is this about putting words down on paper?

Bingo.

Struggling to Put Words on Paper

Putting something in writing—committing words to paper or computer screen—has always been a struggle. Even writing thank-you notes or notes of appreciation is difficult and gets delayed far too long.

The moment you hit the "send" button, you can't take it back.

Recently I confided my difficulty in putting words to paper to a few people. To my amazement there was immediate recognition.

"Yes!" each affirmed, "This is a huge problem. Putting words down for others to see feels like I'm making a commitment." And, they added, "I thought I was the only one with this problem."

I thought this was MY fear, MY incapacity, MY paralysis. I guess I'm not alone. Putting words on paper brings up all kinds of fears.

It may be Fear of Rejection or Failure or Success for some.

It may be Fear of Visibility or Disappointment or Judgment for others. It may be all of them.

And What About You?

Have you, too, faced confusion or fear about taking on new challenges?

When conflicting ideas lead to uncertainty and confusion, calling a "time-out" with yourself lets you step away and sort things out. As you understand your fear and ambivalence, you can see your options more clearly.

Taking a step back can give you the space to move forward.

The Voices Quiet Down

The voices of MY Fear Team are more subdued. They still try to taunt me, but I pay little attention:

"You say you know just what to do.
We say you don't. So who are you?"

I'm discovering who I am as I go through the process of facing these kinds of challenges.

I'm Elayne Savage. I have something to say.

And I just hit the "send" button.

Elayne Savage, Ph.D., is a professional speaker, workplace coach, psychotherapist, and the author of *Breathing Room— Creating Space to be a Couple* and *Don't Take It Personally! The Art of Dealing with Rejection*. She lives in Berkeley, CA and can be

contacted through her website www.QueenofRejection.com
Twitter@ElayneSavage
LinkedIn.com/in/elaynesavage

* * * * * *

Some people face great fear about starting a business. You can *get your fear to quiet down* when you start studying the best practices for making your new business a success. Along this line, I'm now sharing an article from Rebecca Morgan.

Stellar Customer Service In Action
by Rebecca Morgan, CSP, CMC

Many organizations say they strive to deliver stellar customer service, but few empower their employees to deliver the actions that make the organization stand out. Following are three stories of organizations that hired exemplars and allowed them to work their customer service magic.

Small kindnesses create customer loyalty

While staying at the Borei Ankor Resort in Siem Reap, Cambodia, I enjoyed getting to know the staff. Many of them stood out as having exemplary guest service skills. Sometimes it was those without fancy titles who made my stay most memorable.

While ordering a drink at the bar I couldn't help but notice the beautiful lilies the bartender was arranging for the hors d'oeuvre table. I said, "I love how those lilies smell." He smiled and said, "Would you like some for your room?" Of course I said yes!

His gesture brought me joy every day as I looked at and smelled the small bouquet of lilies adorning my room. It cost the hotel nothing as these flowers had been from a wedding in their ballroom earlier that day. Yet his thoughtfulness created a warm feeling of loyalty for me and this beautiful resort.

What can your people offer that doesn't cost you a thing, but creates loyalty in your customers?

Patience shows exemplary service

I needed to have a document not only notarized, but "medallion-ized," which only the manager or assistant manager can do at my credit union. I called the manager to make sure he'd be there when I arrived and we set a time to meet.

At the appointed time I arrived only to learn he was at another branch! I didn't know he served two branches and he didn't mention where he'd be, thus the mix up. His assistant called him and he instructed me to see Elva, the assistant manager.

Elva was very helpful, but said she'd need to see a recent statement for the account, as she was attesting to the funds in the account. The manager hadn't asked for a statement for another account I'd had "medallion-ized" a few weeks earlier. I was the beneficiary of the account, not the account holder, so I was a bit miffed as it meant I'd need to get it and return.

I returned a few days later. This time, Elva read the documents more carefully. She discovered I also needed my father's death certificate, which of course I didn't have.

However, we wanted to verify this was really needed before I traipsed off once again.

So we called Franklin Templeton (where the account was held) and talked to the patient and courteous Stacy Base. Stacy confirmed that I did need the death certificate and helped us with some other details that were confusing. After assisting us in many areas, she connected us to a colleague who was an expert on other parts of our questions.

When I returned with the death certificate, Elva medallion-ized the document and I was done in moments.

I was impressed with not only Elva's patience in helping me through the confusion and offering to call Franklin Templeton, but her willingness to do some hand holding along the way.

- If you are in two sites, do you communicate clearly where you'll meet your client?
- Are your people willing to call a third party to help out a customer, or do they just tell the customer to call and get back to them?
- Do your people help with a little handholding to help a customer in a confusing situation?

Going beyond boundaries to wow the customer

I expected the brief 1-hour flight from Penang, Malaysia to Singapore to be uneventful. Instead, however, I was treated to anther example of Singapore Airlines above-and-beyond service.

The flight was reasonably empty, so I took the opportunity to ask the lead steward how he liked the new uniforms SIA had just rolled out. Instead of different colored suit jackets to denote the stewards' rank, they all now wore dark blue suits and their ties were color-coded to their status.

He was affable, as most SIA cabin crew are. He explained how the stewards' ties now coordinated with the stewardess' (their name for flight attendants) dresses. His tie was green, which meant he was a lead steward, and the lead stewardess's dress had a green background.

He good-naturedly asked how I liked the suits. I said the stewards always looked sharp. He said, "What about the tie?" I smiled, saying it looked classy. Seeing that I was playful, he then asked, "And what about my hair?" We both laughed as I said I liked his short-cropped curly hair.

Which then began a laugh-infused conversation about how he didn't like his curly hair, and I shared how my hair, too, was naturally wavy and I often straightened it. We schmoozed for a few minutes.

He disappeared, then reappeared calling me by name. He must have looked me up on the passenger list. He asked if he could get me anything else, and I jokingly said, "Chocolate?" knowing these short flights didn't often have treats like that, and rarely in coach.

A few minutes later he and a stewardess appeared with a plate of four chocolate cookies on a silver platter. When I delightedly asked if they got them from First Class, they said yes. So he purloined a treat from another class just to make me happy!

We joked and laughed the rest of the flight. I gave him my card and he said he would buy my book *Calming Upset Customers*.

Soon the steward manager came by and introduced himself. He asked about my book and my philosophy on customer service and if I was available to speak to groups. Of course I am!

This was just another example of how SIA turned an everyday encounter into a memorable experience. Even if he hadn't produced chocolate, the interaction with the steward would have made my day.

Rebecca L. Morgan, CSP, CMC, specializes in creating innovative solutions for customer service challenges. She's appeared on *60 Minutes, Oprah, the Wall Street Journal, National Public Radio* and *USA Today*. Rebecca is the bestselling author of 25 books, including *Calming Upset Customers* and *Professional Selling*. She is an exemplary resource who partners with you to accomplish high ROI on your strategic customer service projects. For information on her services, books, and resources, or for permission to repost or reprint this article, contact her at 408/998-7977,
Rebecca@RebeccaMorgan.com,
http://www.RebeccaMorgan.com/

* * * * * *

For those who start a business or have an interest in doing so, there is a reality: You will need to lead yourself and to lead others. Now, I'm sharing crucial management and leadership practices from Chip Conley:

The 5 Fundamentals of Management Etiquette
by Chip Conley

"Should I go to business school?" I hear this question all the time. There's not an easy answer as there are so many variables that are unique to each person. But, more and more, I'm giving a simple piece of advice to those who ask. I don't know whether getting an MBA is meant for you, but I can assure you that if you live by these 5 basic rules of management etiquette, you will succeed in your career, probably beyond your wildest dreams.

In general, I'm not much into etiquette and am a rule-breaker and rebel by nature. But, there's something to be said for common sense when it comes to human nature. So, rather than thinking of this as etiquette, just think of these suggestions as habits that can help you to become more emotionally intelligent and successful.

1. Get an "A" for Attention. The wisdom traditions have long stated that life is all about where you pay your attention. This is true in business as well. Learning to be an intentional listener such that you are truly hearing the other person (rather than just preparing your response) will serve you whether you're in a company with those you work for or with those who work for you. Better yet, be curious about what's the motivation behind what the person is saying. Inquire with a few respectful, but unique questions that help the other person feel they've been heard and that might give them some insight about themselves. Mother Teresa said, "The greatest disease in the West today is not TB or leprosy; it is being unwanted, unloved, and uncared for." Receiving real attention is what we all starve for.

2. Be Radically Responsive. After two-dozen-years of being the CEO of a hospitality company with more than a half-million customers staying in our hotels and a million customers eating at our restaurants, I know a bit about fielding complaints calls. Here's my responsiveness rule: within 15-20 minutes after learning of a call, letter, or email that expresses a complaint (this is true for upset employees

as well), I respond. Clearly, I may have none of the facts to engage in an extended conversation, but it makes a huge difference if I say (in a few short sentences): "I'm sorry about what happened and let me look into it further and either I or the manager of that business will respond to you within 24 or 48 hours" (depending upon the situation). That potential "terrorist" who was about to spread all kinds of ugly comments about your business on social media sites now feels respected and when you try to come to a resolution in a later conversation, the upset person is in a better frame of mind.

3. Remember the "little" things. When I'm doing emotional intelligence workshops in companies, we do an exercise in which we ask for the qualities that defined people's most and least admired bosses. The most common quality I hear is, "My boss always asked how my son and daughter were doing and he remembered their names." or "I received a nice email early in the morning on my birthday from my boss." What may seem little to you means the world to someone else. There are many methods to keep track of these little things. Just know that this is a BIG thing so you better find the method that helps you to be good at this.

4. Under-promise and Over-deliver. Disappointment = Expectations − Reality. Whether it's Facebook's IPO nose-dive or that vacation resort that looked so good on the internet but turned out to be a pig sty, we keep a report card in our head of who's delighted us and who's disappointed us. This is particularly true in project-based business environments, especially when there's a domino effect with under-delivering. Again, not delivering on a promise is a

different form of disrespect from the perspective of the person who's been disappointed. Lastly, if you know you're going to miss your promise, manage expectations as early as you can in the process because missing the promise and surprising your boss is a combustible combination.

5. Practice Gratitude. Social scientists have found that the fastest way to feel happiness is to practice gratitude. Feeling good about your life, but not expressing a heartfelt "thank you" is like wrapping a gift for someone and never giving it to them. Here re three habits that can make this an on-going, powerful practice in your work life: (a) Make a rule of giving gratitude twice a day at work and if you miss Monday, you need to do four on Tuesday; (b) If possible, express the gratitude in person or in a fashion in which the person can really hear your authentic appreciation; and (c) Be as specific as possible about why this was meaningful to you because just saying "you did a great job" doesn't create a profound moment of learning for the other person.

CHIP CONLEY

Hotel guru. Armchair psychologist. Traveling philosopher. Author. Speaker. Teacher. Student.

Chip Conley has lived out more than one calling in his lifetime.

Founder and former CEO of Joie de Vivre (JDV), Chip has led the development, creation, and management of more boutique hotels than anyone else in the world. Starting JDV at age 26, his mission was to "create joy" by building a company that USA Today called "the most delightfully schizophrenic collection of hotels in America." During his 24 years as CEO, JDV grew to become the second largest boutique hotel company in America.

Chip shares his unique prescription for success in *PEAK: How Great Companies Get Their Mojo from Maslow*, based on noted psychologist Abraham Maslow's iconic Hierarchy of Needs. The

New York Times bestseller, *EMOTIONAL EQUATIONS: Simple Truths for Creating Happiness + Success*, is Chip's latest book where he takes us from emotional intelligence to emotional fluency—placing meaning at the top of the balance sheet. His previous books include *The Rebel Rules: Daring to be Yourself in Business*, and *Marketing That Matters: 10 Practices to Profit Your Business and Change the World*. Chip presents his theories on transformation and meaning—in business and life—to audiences around the world and he's been a featured speaker at TED.

Honored with the 2012 Pioneer Award—hospitality's highest accolade—The San Francisco Business Times named Chip the Most Innovative CEO—and JDV the 2 in the entire Bay Area. Chip received his BA and MBA from Stanford University and holds an Honorary Doctorate in Psychology from Saybrook University, where he is the 2012/2013 ScholarPractitioner in residence. He served on the Glide Memorial Board for nearly a decade and is now on the Boards of the Burning Man Project, the Esalen Institute, and Youth Speaks.

Chip's latest calling is traveling the globe—speaking about transformative business practices and seeking out the world's best festivals. He's on a mission to cultivate more cultural curiosity by sharing the "collective effervescence" found in the festival experience. Chip's travel blog is at FEST300.com and he is also AFAR magazine's festival correspondent at AFAR.com.

www.chipconley.com

* * * * *

Becoming successful in business requires that we stay up with the times. Now, Danek S. Kaus shares insights about podcasts, Twitter and persuasive language.

Create Your Success through Podcasts, Using Twitter Well, and Persuasive Language
by Danek S. Kaus

Podcasts:

7 Reasons Why Being a Guest on Podcasts Will Help You Get Free Publicity

Many people who have an interest in being a guest on radio talk shows think that being on podcasts or internet radio shows is a waste of time. A few years ago, this was probably true.

But many of these internet radio shows have garnered followings large enough to interest big-name authors, singers, actors and athletes. Even shows with relatively small audiences can help you market yourself for free. Just look at the main page of Blogtalk.com and look at the pictures of upcoming guests that rotate on the page.

With that said, here are seven reasons why appearing on these shows is a good way to get free publicity.

1. Many of them have loyal listeners. The shows are often based on a particular topic, so people with an interest tune in and subscribe.

2. They have active listeners. Because they have an interest in the topic, they pay attention. In traditional radio talk shows, people are often doing other things, such as driving somewhere, making dinner, etc. You may only have their partial attention, which means only a small part of your message is heard and even less is acted upon. Some in the

audience may have no interest at all in your topic. They may be a fan of the host and are merely tolerating you.

3. It's a good way to practice your skills. If you're new to being interviewed, you can make your mistakes in front of a smaller group of people. And keep in mind, these listeners are more interested in what you have to say as opposed to how you say it.

4. These shows tend to have longevity. Although many broadcast radio shows do archive their interviews on the Internet, many do not. Those that do archive them, often keep them for a limited time. Podcasts tend to stay on the web for years. Listeners can also download the shows to their hard drive or MP3 player.

5. They are searchable. People interested in a certain topic can search for podcasts by key words. So once again, they are listened to by people with a sincere interest in the topic, which can translate to more business or other benefits for you, in addition to the free publicity.

6. You could get lucky. For example, a book editor who works for a large publishing house might be a fan of the show and offer you a book deal. A listener might offer you a chance to speak at their next convention. Or you might establish a long-term relationship with the host that can be mutually beneficial.

7. Some podcasts have large audiences. Some internet shows have over 100,000 listeners all over the world. Imagine what that could do for your reputation and image.

* * *

Use Twitter Well:

Want a Huge Twitter Following? Here's How to Get More Twitter Followers

If you're on Twitter you know what a powerful marketing tool it can be. But the key to success is finding and keeping followers. Here are 11 steps you can take to get more Twitter followers.

1. Create a great Twitter bio. One of the key factors in whether or not people decide to follow you is the quality of the information in your bio. If you have a relevant website, be sure to include the URL. You only have 160 characters, as opposed to the 140 allowed in tweets, so use them well.

2. If you're new to Twitter, create about 10 or so interesting tweets before looking for followers. You have to give people a reason to want to follow you.

3. If you find an interesting article on the web, tweet about it with a link. Because most links will be too long, you can shorten them by going to tinyurl.com. Simply paste in the old link and it will give you a new "tiny" link to use for free.

4. Tweet inspiring or humorous quotes. You can find a lot of great quotes that your Twitter followers will enjoy at BrainyQuotes.com

5. Tweet links to interesting videos from YouTube and other such sites.

6. Help others by re-tweeting their tweets. Many will return the favor, which will expose you to other people who may then decide to follow you.

7. Join the conversation. Reply to other people's tweets, give them a compliment or thank them for sharing. These people may also decide to send you @ messages, which will also make their followers aware of you.

8. Thank people who re-tweet you. Just hit the reply button and send a thank-you note. If you don't thank them, at least some of the time, they will probably stop re-tweeting you and stop following you.

9. Become active on Follow Friday. Each Friday, recommend some of your favorite tweeters to your followers by typing in #FollowFriday or #FF and then their Twitter handle, such as @JaneSmith. Others will do the same for you. This is a great way to get more Twitter Followers.

10. Follow all of Twitter's rule about following and un-following. Don't become too aggressive or your account will be suspended.

11. If you are marketing something, try to keep a ratio of about one marketing message for every 10 or so tweets. If all you do is try to sell people something, they will stop following you. Doing nothing but marketing tweets could get you labeled as a spammer, which could result in being banned. Remember Twitter is about being social first and marketing, if you do any marketing, second.

* * *

Use Persuasive Language:
"Crazy Like a Fox, Persuasive Like a Weasel"

Imagine the power of using hidden commands in normal conversation to increase sales, convince others to do something or to accept your ideas. This is often done by separating out a simple command or suggestion by pausing, stating the command in a different tone of voice, then resuming normal conversation.

For example, when selling a car you might say, "This car gets 30 miles per gallon on the highway, which you'll notice when you (pause) take it for a test drive. You'll also notice that ...."

Another way to insert a command into conversation is to use what are called Weasel Words. These phrases are based on the one of the techniques used by Milton Erickson, who was one of the foremost hypnotists of the last century. Erickson had a way of talking people into trance without giving any direct commands to close their eyes or relax. Instead he would just sort of talk around the idea of going into trance and people would naturally do it.

These Ericksonian Phrases are also known as Weasel Words because they allow you to weasel in a command without it being so direct or authoritarian. For example, you might say to someone, "Consider why you want to do this."

With some people, giving a command can create a great deal of resistance. A percentage of them just do not like to take orders so they won't respond to direct suggestion.

But what if your were to say, "I'm not entirely sure how well you can consider why you want to do this." Here, you're not trying to force them to consider why. You're just asking them how well they might be able to consider why.

Now, in considering and interpreting that statement the mind has to actually consider why they want to do this, to some degree. When you use Weasel Words the listener does not have something to object to. In order to employ these phrases you first determine your outcome.

In a hypnosis setting, one outcome would be for the client to relax. You might say, "A friend once told me, you know, it's entirely possible to just get relaxed." You're not telling the client to relax. You're just repeating what a friend once said.

If you're selling computers, you might say something like, "I wonder if now is the time that you might buy this computer." There are hundreds of Ericksonian Phrases that can be used for just about any outcome. Here are a few below. You can probably come up with your many of your own.

WEASEL WORDS

After you come to ... After you've ... As a whole new way of thinking opens up ... All that really matters ... All that's really important ... Allowing yourself to just naturally ... And as that occurs, you really can't help but notice ... And I'd like to have you discover ... And then, now you'll discover ... And you can be pleased .... And you can really use it ... And you can wonder ... And you will be surprised at ... Give yourself the opportunity to see if ... I wonder if you'll be pleased to notice ... I wonder if you'll be reminded ... I wonder if you'll be surprised to discover that ... In all probability ... If you could ... It is easy, isn't it ... Perhaps you wouldn't mind noticing ... So now's the time ...

Danek S. Kaus is the author of *You Can Be Famous! Insider Secrets to Getting Free Publicity*. He has helped people to get featured in *USA Today*, CNN, *the New York Times* and hundreds of other newspapers, radio and TV shows and magazines. Get more publicity tips at www.freepublicityforyou.com

* * * * * *

To love yourself means you take good care of yourself. You'll need your reserves of energy and well being so that you stretch and do what's necessary to increase your financial abundance.

BOOK TWO:
LOVE YOURSELF TO SPIRITUAL JOY

Have you ever been cut down by a friend or family member and just wanted to shake off the pain and get on with your life? We'll explore three truths that will nurture you.

1. Spiritual Joy is in this present moment.
Earlier today, I went to see my father and mother. They live in another city some distance from me. My mother is a kind, generous soul and I wonder how she got burdened with my father who seems to become more bitter with each passing year.

My sweetheart proclaimed today that she never wants to be in the presence of my father again.

I can empathize with that.

The rude and mean comments that my father said today remind me that Spiritual Joy is in this present moment. How?

My interaction with my father is *in the past*.

I have a choice right now as to what I do. Sure a painful thought may arise; my choice is in my next thought. So I now choose to have better moments as I write this article. I find comfort and insight as I write. I also find meaning in sharing helpful ideas with my readers. Before today, I had expected to complete and post a different article at my blog. But now this material feels relevant and timely.

We have a choice with each moment: To make the most of this moment or to get lost in pain or regret of the past. Or to be twisted by worries for the future. Either way, we step out of the present moment.

You see my father's cut-down remarks of today echo how he'd throw me into walls when I was a boy.

The difference is that as a man I now chose to end the conversation. When his remarks were too much, I simply said, "We're done," and I stepped away from him. My father left the building.

In that instant, I chose my next moment. Away from my father, I sat with my sweetheart and my mother and we had some good moments together.

2. Become skilled to *return* to the present moment.

Many spiritual paths emphasize deep breathing, prayer or quiet time to bring us into the present moment.

As I write these words, I take deep breaths, allowing my belly to expand on inhaling. I exhale and allow my belly to deflate.

Try three such breaths now, and see how you start to feel more calm.

Another method of returning to the present moment is embodied in the phrase: "I don't run that show." I use this phrase to remind myself that there is much I do not control. I do not control my father's bitterness. I do not control that my kind mother is married to someone who routinely says to her and me, "You make me mad."

An old phrase is: "You teach people how to treat you." Today, I ended a conversation in which my father berated me. That action may or may not help.

Still I make choices as best as I can, and I remind myself "I don't run that show."

Why is it important to return to the present moment? It's where you can experience joy. Also, if you're clear of past pain, you can respond to opportunities in the present moment.

When you answer the knock of opportunity, you need your bags already packed. – Tom Marcoux

3. Compassion is the answer.

Some definitions of compassion include "recognizing another's pain with the desire to relieve it."

Imagine that you truly love yourself. What would that mean?

Would you allow yourself to be imperfect?

I'll put this another way. What would you say to your best friend if he or she was going through a difficulty?

Wouldn't you be kind? Wouldn't you suggest that your friend take care of himself or herself?

Sure you would.

I'm inviting you to look upon your own pain with the same compassion.

Give yourself what you need.

Further, I invite you to explore how you release yourself from painful feelings. Forgiveness actually frees the person who forgives.

I choose at this time to avoid cutting off interaction with

my father.

The next time I see him he may address me with berating words—or not.

I'll see what happens when I get there.

I call this *enter the moment fresh*.

When I see my father the next time, will I respond to his berating words with "We're done" or will I listen for a time?

I'll enter the moment fresh.

And I'll remember that compassion toward myself and to others will be a helpful guideline.

Compassion helps us experience spiritual joy.

Now, we'll explore the following topics:

1. How You Can Overcome Obstacles to Your Happiness
2. How You Can "Source By Divine Love"
3. How You can LOVE Your Life
4. Where Your Real Freedom Is—And How You Can Experience It!
5. How You Can Get Free of Emotional Pain
6. Under Pressure?–Here's What Can Really Help You (something better than "Be Optimistic")

* * * * * *

Topic #1:
Book Two: Love Yourself to Spiritual Joy

How You Can Overcome Obstacles to Your Happiness

Do you feel burdened by obstacles to your happiness? We'll become stronger and learn about F.E.A.R.S.:

F - fear
E - expectation
A - approval
R - resistance (judgment)
S - "stressed-out identity"

1. Fear

Avoid letting fear run your big decisions. Why? Because your life will be severely limited. Let's look at two "voices:"
- *Voice of Fear:* contract, do not take a risk, hide
- *Voice of Intuition:* expand, take an appropriate risk, experiment, express creativity, shine.

Consider heeding the voice of intuition.

To heed the voice of intuition, you pause and notice if you feel a form of yearning. Do you have an impression that gives you a bit of thrill? Are you thinking "what if I try that?" Don't let that spark die.

Meanwhile . . . fear does have a good use. I once wrote: "Fear keeps you on the mountain. Use it as a springboard for preparation and staying vigilant."

Choose what you really want. Then get coaching, learn new skills and rehearse to develop new methods and reflexes to perform better. In other words, do what it takes to get what you really want.

2. Expectation

Holding tight to expectations can create more miserable moments. Why? The world often presents situations that simply go against our preferences. It's helpful to be open to whatever good is present in your current reality. I always remember author John Gray's story of how "Julia," one of his clients, was miserable that her mother treated her poorly. By focusing on her mother's behavior, Julia failed to treasure her aunt who was consistently kind to her and functioned as a surrogate mother. Julia's mother avoided her, but Julia's aunt invited her over for the holiday season.

It's understandable to have thoughts and feelings of sadness around a terrible parent. YET, we can ask ourselves: "What else is good in my life? What else is possible?"

Let go of expectations and make the best of what you have. You'll enjoy more happy moments.

3. Approval

By accident, my father taught me something important about approval: *It's important to NOT live for others' approval.* The reason is that many people, like my father, attempt to use approval to control another person's behavior.

I'm glad that I developed the courage and insight to go my own way, regardless of the lack of approval from my father. My father has admitted that he is a man of little imagination. He could *not* imagine doing anything like being a feature film director or entrepreneur—paths that I'm on. But he withheld approval and always had a critical opinion about subjects for which he had no experience.

I invite you to be careful about other people's opinions. It's better to seek the counsel of people who have *actually accomplished* what you want to do.

By the way, here's something that I've noticed. When I have gone my own way and accomplished something, a disapproving family member or friend would simply shrug and say, "Oh, I guess I was wrong." The point here is that it did ***not*** matter much to that person if his disapproval may have denied me the joy of creativity and even financial abundance to handle financial obligations.

Again, do NOT live for others' approval.

4. Resistance (judgment)

A number of people I've met lose a lot of personal energy to resisting things in their lives. Some people stand like a rock in the middle a coursing river, complaining about the water slamming into them. Others live much like a canoe, flowing with the river and choosing the ports that they visit.

The idea is to pick where you want to go (like the canoe).

Perhaps, you feel that saving 10% of every income check you earn is a good idea. Often, you'll probably get nowhere trying to convince all of your friends of the soundness of that habit. Let it go. Walk your own path.

A number of philosophical books talk about the importance of acceptance as a mode of living. I can understand the value of accepting life and people as they are—as a first step to letting go.

However, to "accept" something, it is likely that you once judged it as "wrong." That's a lot of energy. In essence, you set up your own resistance.

Instead, you can choose "awareness." When you see something that is not to your preference, you merely label it as "different." You are *aware* that it is different. You do not waste energy in labeling it as wrong. We're talking about non-harmful things here. For example, I appreciate songs of various types of music. I've met older people who say that the creation of good music stopped at the year 1959.

To many, that might seem to be an extreme opinion.

And, this becomes an opportunity to merely label that narrow definition of good music as "different." I will *avoid* wasting a moment trying to convince the older person about the value of contemporary music.

5. "Stressed-out identity"

Where does your identity come from? Is your identity based on something you can control? Like what you do and what you personally focus on?

I once based my identity on my long friendships. Then I was shocked when two thirty-year-long friendships disappeared from my life.

With both people, I spent hour after hour listening to their concerns and upsets. I was surprised that the two people ultimately did not value such attentive listening on my part.

You see I had built my identity on how kind and compassionate I was in friendship.

In fact, twenty minutes before one friend left my life, he said, "I never said you weren't a good listener."

Now, my identity is about being kind *in the moment* and being supportive in *the moment.* I let go of the idea of "long friendships as proof of my being a good friend and a good person."

People come and go. Some people stay. Some relationships are novels, others are shorts stories, and some are a sentence.

Pick for your identity your own values and what you can personally do.

You'll reduce your own stress. You'll create more moments of happiness.

* * *

A lot of opportunities for happiness are choked by fears. Let's briefly look at the F.E.A.R.S.

F - fear [enough said.]

E - expectation [We fear that our expectations will not be met and that we won't get what we want.]

A - approval [We fear that we'll lose someone's approval and that we may lose their love and acceptance.]

R - resistance (judgment) [We fear that if someone chooses to go against our preferences we'll lose out on what we want.]

S - "stressed-out identity" [We fear, subconsciously, that we may fall apart if what we base our identity on (perhaps, a marriage or friendship) suddenly goes away.]

To be locked up in FEARS can cause us to make faulty choices that cut off our feeling fully alive.

Stay aware of FEARS and *still make choices that support your aliveness.*

You'll find happiness on a journey of aliveness.

* * * * * *

Life can be rough. So it helps to be able to bring the joy and relief of humor and laughter into tough times. Along this line, I'm now sharing an article from Allen Klein.

Love's A Funny Thing
by Allen Klein, MA, CSP (aka Mr. Jollytologist®)

"Avoid humorless people-and do not marry one, for God's sake." - Garrison Keillor

Most people, I am guessing, think of love as serious. Yet, when women were asked what they wanted in a potential mate, one of the most important things was that the man had to have a good sense of humor.

Maybe it is because women intuitively know that couples who can laugh together can weather the trials and tribulations that life inevitably brings.

I know one couple, for example, who hide red sponge-rubber clown noses around the house. When an argument breaks out, one of them dons the nose and, like a red-light at an intersection, the potential fight is stopped in its tracks.

A friend of mine, who is a therapist, also told me how she uses another fun prop with some couples in conflict. Recently, a woman complained about how insensitive her husband was. For nearly an entire session she harped on his saying there was lint in her belly-button when they were making love the previous night. To help the woman let go and lighten up about this incident, the therapist asked both of them to don Groucho glasses and resume their lint-filled conversation.

As soon as the giggling started, the complaining stopped.

And finally, a colleague of mine, sent me an amusing story, which illustrates how a little humor can make a big point.

Although this married couple enjoyed their new fishing boat together, it was the husband who was behind the wheel operating the boat. He was concerned about what might happen in an emergency. So one day, out on the lake he said to his wife, "Please take the wheel, dear. Pretend that I am having a heart attack. You must get the boat safely to shore and dock it."

So she drove the boat to shore and safely docked it.

Later that evening, the wife walked into the living room where her husband was watching television. She sat down next to him, switched the TV channel, and said to him,

"Please go into the kitchen, dear. Pretend I'm having a heart attack and set the table, cook dinner and wash the dishes."

Allen Klein, aka "Mr. Jollytologist", is an award-winning professional speaker who shows audiences worldwide how to find and use humor to deal with changes, challenges, and not-so-funny stuff. He is a recipient of a Lifetime Achievement Award from the Association for Applied and Therapeutic Humor, a Toastmaster's Communication and Leadership Award, a Certified Speaking Professional designation from the National Speaker's Association and a Hunter College (NYC) Hall of Fame honoree. Klein is also the best-selling author of such books as *The Healing Power of Humor, Learning to Laugh When You Feel Like Crying,* and *The Art of Living Joyfully,* among others.

Contact: humor@allenklein.com or www.allenklein.com

* * * * * *

Topic #2
(Book Two: Love Yourself to Spiritual Joy)
How You Can "Source By Divine Love"

Want a source to feel better and more hopeful? We'll use the S.E.E. process.

S – source daily by Divine Love
E – erase the ego
E – engage

1. Source daily by Divine Love
To source is to get something from a particular place. What place? I suggest a place outside of depending on others to hold you up.

Where do you get your energy from? If you only feel good when you accomplish something or when someone approves of you, you may find yourself in an "energy crisis."

Instead, consider doing something each day to connect with your Divine Source. For over a decade, I've been teaching Comparative Religion on the college level. And I've observed that a number of spiritual paths suggest that a person pray or meditate to connect with a Divine Source.

My clients report that they
- meditate for 10 minutes in the morning
- go for a walk at a park at lunchtime
- pray
- practice deep breathing

To "source daily by Divine Love" is to make a bit of time and space to turn your perspective to an expansive level. What is the alternative? Many of us find it easy to settle for the perspective of "clod of ailments" as George Bernard Shaw mentioned in this quote:

This is the true joy in life, the being used for a purpose recognized by yourself as a mighty one; the being a force of nature instead of a feverish, selfish little clod of ailments and grievances complaining that the world will not devote itself to making you happy. - George Bernard Shaw

To "source by Divine Love" is to hold that there IS Divine Love. If your heart resonates with that idea, you may find great comfort that the goodness of the universe supports you. Also, you would likely feel renewed after a session of meditating, praying and/or walking in a park.

2. Erase the ego

A number of authors have suggested that the ego is made of fear and that we cannot "erase the ego—that part of us that feels small and vulnerable."

However, you CAN erase the tyranny of the ego *in the moment*. How? By choosing your next thought. The first thought you have in a situation may automatically arise from your ego. But you can pre-condition yourself to think an empowering thought as the next thought.

For example, I know someone who has buckets full of compassion for pets and a teaspoon full of compassion for people. My first train of thought is: "This is wrong. People are important. I'd like to see compassion shown for me and my troubles."

My second train of thought that I have pre-chosen is: "It is as it is. This person is different. I do not run this show."

Do you see how my second train of thought can calm me down and release me from the strain of my first thoughts' judgmental properties?

By pre-planning my second train of thought, I am free to go on and enjoy the rest of my day.

3. Engage

I'm writing a musical in which one character drops people when they become inconvenient to her. By this pattern, she cannot know real love because love involves supporting others even when you're in discomfort. Love is not where you go to get; it's where you go to give.

To experience the blessing of love, you need to engage in loving actions.

I have thought a lot about compassion which is part of love.

If you want other people to be happy,
practice compassion.
If you want to be happy,
practice compassion. – The Dalai Lama

And I realized that a number of people fail to practice compassion because it hurts.

It is taking on another person's hurt to some extent.

When I hear of some tragedy that a person is suffering, I sometimes reply, "I grieve with you." Pain often results from loss. So I'm acknowledging the person's loss.

I pause and pay attention. I allow myself to feel empathy even though it causes me to feel pain.

I know some people who are too quick to offer some facile solution with thoughtless comments like: "You're young. You'll find another husband." The person offering this comment has failed to engage—they have failed to be truly present for the other person.

I invite you to engage in the moment. Be present with people. Allow yourself to feel empathy. You'll experience a new level of connection.

In summary, remember to SEE:
- Source daily by Divine Love
- Erase the ego
- Engage

Your value is beyond any accomplishment or others' approval.

Your value is recognized by your Divine Source.

Connect with your Divine Source and feel a level of peace and happiness beyond the petty human conundrums of daily life.

* * * * * *

Topic #3
(Book Two: Love Yourself to Spiritual Joy)
How You can LOVE Your Life

Are you barely hanging on? Do you wonder where your zest for living went? We'll use the F.R.E.E. process:

F – fuel
R – release
E – excitement
E – engagement

1. Fuel

When you want to feel free and enjoy your life, you'll make sure that you have enough "fuel." Without appropriate nutrition and sleep, you're running on near empty. It just doesn't work. How do you get enough sleep? I'll share what I do: I keep a log. When I see that I have missed some sleep, I take steps to get more sleep on the next day.

Be sure you have enough fuel so that you feel good and strong. Exercise forms part of your "fueling system." Regular exercise actually adds to your personal energy.

I find that reading is fuel to me. I stay excited about ideas and ways to help my graduate students, clients and readers of my own books.

2. Release

Life can be tough. Things happen and you feel burdened by painful feelings. You simply need time to release the painful feelings and experience the good side of life.

Another way to say this is: "Plan your release." What is a release? It's something that you do to expel painful energy.

Exercise helps many of us release the stress we feel.

I purposely get laughter-time daily. I watch stand-up comedy moments on YouTube or view comedy-related DVDs/Blu-ray discs. Everyday.

Many of us find that quiet time or moments for spiritual connection (prayer; meditation) to be helpful.

3. Excitement

Are you just going through the motions? Are you dragging through life? It's important to notice your daily mood and approach to life. And then do something to put more life into your life.

Unfortunately, a number of people allow themselves to fall into and remain in a rut. I've asked a number of people, "What are you looking forward to?" Two people routinely had nothing to say. One of them even resented that I asked the question. That guy is no longer part of my life (his choice)—and what a relief! What a miserable person!

But this is NOT for you.

Doing the same thing day in and day out can create the feeling of "blah."

On the other hand, you have the choice to make something enjoyable and exciting take place.

Here's a principle that I use: Make it a game that you can win.

Many people allow themselves to fall into a frustrating pattern of trying to control the actions of others. They complain about their disappointments; and they're engaged in a game that they cannot win.

But we can control our own efforts. For example, I recently decided: "Today is the day I finish my new book." And in that same day, I had my book up on Amazon.com as a Kindle book.

It was exciting for me to watch with anticipation for the time the book went "live" on Amazon.com.

Along this line, here are other principles for bringing some excitement to your life:
- Push on through so that you can succeed somewhere. (Even a small success can give you the energy boost to keep going.)
- Aim for more than one thing.
- Have something new coming up.
- Enjoy today AND have something you look forward to.

Happiness is pretty simple: someone to love, something to do, something to look forward to. – Rita Mae Brown

4. Engagement

I always remember a book I read as I completed my degree in psychology. The author Irvin Yalom proposed that the solution to the problems of life is one thing: Engagement. What does that mean? Get connected! Get involved!

Over several years, I have faced some tough times. (The suicide of a close friend is one of them.)

One powerful way I stay engaged is to make sure to make a contribution to the well being of other people. For example, when I talk about my work coaching graduate students and clients, I say, "I'm grateful for meaningful work."

Perhaps, at the moment, you're not pressing to find a job that's more in line with your deepest heart. Then, consider setting up a situation so that you can say something like: "I'm grateful for my meaningful volunteer work on Saturdays."

Or "I'm grateful for my meaningful hobby."

So I've learned that a powerful part of engagement is having something to feel grateful about and to have some way to contribute to the well-being of another person.

In writing 22 books, I have stayed engaged with serving the well being of my readers. I write everyday, so regardless of how the day goes, I know that I have had a personal victory in writing—even just a paragraph. I'm excited that my new book *Secrets of Awesome Dinner Guests: What Walt Disney, Steve Jobs, Oprah Winfrey, Albert Einstein, Martin Luther King, Jr., Helen Keller, and John Lasseter Can Teach You About Success and Fulfillment* is now available at Amazon.com. I share this detail because I consciously choose to create enjoyable and exciting moments in my life.

Now, I invite you to put into your daily life something that keeps you engaged and feeling good.

Answer this question: "What's the ONE Thing you can do this week such that by doing it everything else would be easier or unnecessary?" (a question coined by Gary Keller)

I'll add, "What ONE Thing can you do this week that will help you LOVE your life?"

* * * * * *

Topic #4
(Book Two: Love Yourself to Spiritual Joy)
Where Your Real Freedom Is – And How You Can Experience It!

Want to feel free today? We'll use the A.R.E. process.

A - allow
R - relinquish your focus on "the external"
E - enjoy the moment

1. Allow

The idea of "allow" is that you make a choice to "let something just be as it is." The opposite is trying to control just about everything. And that's exhausting. Further, it can be futile.

To feel free in the present moment is to make good choices. Pick what is most important to you. And then, aim to let other things go.

Here's a phrase that I use: "I don't run that show." This is my shorthand way of reminding myself that other people are on their own path and have their own timing.

2. Relinquish your focus on "the external"

Have you heard someone or yourself say, "I'll be happy when I get the new job"?

Then what happens? After a time, the person likely complains about the new job.

I've learned that relying on something external to make me happy can be ultimately disappointing. I remember working for hours in the recording studio to finish a song I wrote. When the work was done, I felt happy and also tired. Over the years, I've learned that it helps to enjoy the moment and to enjoy participating in a project.

Completing a project is like arriving on a temporary plateau. Sure, you feel good for a brief time and then it's onward to whatever life requires.

So don't rely on anything external to "make you happy."

Your actual experience of happiness is in the moment.

You'll experience real freedom when you just take each

moment as it arrives. Squeeze the current moment like an orange to "get the juice."

For example, I'm enjoying discovering each new sentence that I write for this book. Sure, I'll feel some joy upon completing this book, but each moment of the process is really where the experience of joy and freedom resides.

3. Enjoy the moment

Freedom is in this present moment. How can you experience it? It's actually a process of conditioning your mind to come back to the present even though it easily jumps to the future (worries) and the past (regrets).

Here is an example of someone working with her mind.

Audrey wants to feel free in the moment.

Her thoughts flow like this:

"I'd like to feel free now.

How can I feel good now?—I've got that intense job interview tomorrow.

I've rehearsed with three people today.

I can relax now.

How can I relax?

I'll just breathe in deeply and breathe out.

In.

Out.

Relax."

My point here is that Audrey returned her thoughts to the present moment. She assured herself of her previous rehearsal. She avoided letting her thoughts tumble down into a negative spiral.

It helps to pre-plan certain phrases that bring you back to the present.

Here are examples:

- In this moment, I'm fine.
- In this moment, things are working. My family is okay.
- In this moment, I have what I need.

Realize that freedom is not a destination that you achieve for all time.

It's a moment-to-moment personal experience.

Your thoughts can help you make space for the experience of freedom.

Everything can be taken from a man but one thing: the last of the human freedoms—to choose one's attitude in any given set of circumstances, to choose one's own way.
— *Viktor E. Frankl (survivor of Nazi death camps)*

How do we choose our own way? We choose our next thought.

It's certain that some unpleasant thoughts will rise up.

Learn to let them flow past you like a leaf on a stream of water.

Make a deliberate choice of a next thought that empowers you and that gives you space to enjoy the current moment.

* * * * * *

Topic #5
(Book Two: Love Yourself to Spiritual Joy)
How You Can Get Free of Emotional Pain

Would you like to get free of emotional pain and feel stronger? We'll use the H.E.A.L.S. process:

H – hone your thinking
E – express the hurt
A – ask empowering questions
L – let go
S – send it upward

This H.E.A.L.S. process is something I call Productive Processing. It's better than continuously repeating painful thoughts in your mind (which is called negative ruminating).

1. Hone your thinking
Some of us try to dispel the pain by telling our painful story to friends. The problem is that we keep re-stimulating the same neural pathways in the brain.

Instead, what we really need is to create NEW neural pathways.

Sentence Completion
Change your thoughts on a painful topic. Take out a sheet of paper and write down your own unique ways of completing these sentences:
- I am strong after this event because I've learned _____
- I am strong after this event because I know that I can_____

- A good purpose that this event can serve for me and others is _____

2. Express the hurt

I've used a method that I call *Write Down, Rip Up.* You write down what bothers you, and then you rip it up and never read the painful thoughts again. In a way, it is like expelling poison. Rereading what you've written would take the poison back in. So be sure to write it down then rip up the paper.

Another way to feel purged of your painful thoughts is to safely burn the page.

3. Ask empowering questions

Our brains are question-answering devices. Engage the power of your brain by writing down the answers to empowering questions like:
- How can I let go of this?
- How can I let go of this for 30 minutes?
- God, how do I cleanse away the anger, frustration and disappointment? [Some of my clients use the words "Higher Power" or "Spirit."]

4. Let go

One way to let go is to use a form of a Loving-Kindness Meditation.

It is a graduated process. Sit down in a place where you know you'll be free of distractions for five to fifteen minutes.

Practice belly breathing: Breathe in through your nose and out through your mouth. As you inhale, allow your belly to expand and let it deflate as you exhale.

Start by thinking of someone you love.

Think this thought: "[Loved one's name], may your

happiness expand."

After sending these loving thoughts toward people you love, include neutral strangers like: "Clerk at the bookstore, may your happiness expand."

Then, include yourself. "[Say your own name], may your happiness expand."

Finally, as you are able to, think of a person who has wronged you.

Ideally, and eventually, it would be helpful for your well-being for you to add: "[Offending person's name], may your happiness expand."

Here's another technique to let go. Sometimes, I think of a former friend who left under hurtful circumstances. I immediately think, "[Person's Name], blessings to you."

I feel better. I've said a prayer for that person wherever he may be.

And I'm free to go on with my day.

5. Send it upward

For those readers who have a spiritual practice, you might consider using a God Box. Select a pleasant looking box. Write down your painful thoughts, fold up the paper and place the paper into the box, saying a prayer like: "God, this is too big for me. I ask that You take it from me and help me heal. Thank you."

Leave the paper in the box and never re-read it.

* * *

The above methods comprise Productive Processing, which creates new neural pathways. You avoid repeating the same story to different people and to yourself.

Let go of habitual negative thoughts.

Use the methods of Productive Processing and free yourself. You'll also feel more energy to pursue your dreams!

Your freedom and happiness bless this world.

* * * * * *

Topic #6
(Book Two: Love Yourself to Spiritual Joy)
Under Pressure?–Here's What Can Really Help You (something better than "Be Optimistic")

Ever want so much to energize yourself but pressure has really knocked you down? I'll share something real and useful about rising up and feeling stronger.

Recently, I attended a workshop. I agreed with the speaker that optimism is valuable. And I felt there was something missing in the presentation.

If I was giving a speech on optimism, I would likely add: "I imagine that there may a few of us here who feel tired and not optimistic at this moment. If you're feeling that way, I'm with you. I've hit bottom. I've felt drained. In this workshop, I'll share some methods for wherever you find yourself at this moment."

My above words are part of a process I call *Empathy-Plus-One*.

You may notice that I began with empathy for people who do not feel optimistic and who feel tired.

Without empathy, there is no connection with the person where he or she is in this moment.

I've learned that merely proclaiming a good idea (like

"Have optimistic thoughts. Find how the glass is half full") may not be enough when the truth remains that one feels drained.

For example, at this very moment, I have four people in my life who are truly in need:
- one has clinical depression
- another has manic-depressive symptoms
- the third has dementia symptoms
- the forth has congestive heart failure and is facing possible eviction from her home.

They all need support. They want me to provide heartfelt listening and even other forms of assistance.

Frankly, interacting with them can feel draining.

What to do? Show empathy to myself. I must nurture myself.

My process of *Empathy-Plus-One* is:

a) first acknowledge my real feelings and identify where energy is being drained

b) then add a behavior for building energy.

Here's an example of how one's internal thoughts may progress with Empathy-Plus-One:

1) "I should call my depressed friend."

2) How do I feel? How is my energy?

3) I need to "plus one" this. I need to nurture myself. I'll take a 15 minute walk and then call my friend. Then afterward, I'll nurture myself by reading a relaxing book while soaking in a warm bath for 20 minutes.

Do *not* skip the vital step of empathy. Some of us actually lose energy when around someone doing "rah-rah cheerleading." Sometimes, the other person does not have the space or strength to simply hear our hurt feelings. In that case, step away and acknowledge to yourself where you are hurting. You become the accepting companion you crave.

Then add (plus one) something to nurture yourself. [Part of nurturing yourself can be taking gentle care of your personal dreams. For more about making your dream come true, see an Excerpt from my new book *Create Your Best Life: Unleash Your Charisma and Confidence to Change the World*

at http://amzn.to/15I6cD7]

Support your own energy.

* * * * * *

Our conversation about love yourself to spiritual joy continues in the following *Book Three: Secrets of Being Unstoppable—Nonjudgment, Nonresistance and Nonattachment.*

BOOK THREE: SECRETS OF BEING UNSTOPPABLE— NONJUDGMENT, NONRESISTANCE, & NONATTACHMENT

Who can stop you like no one else? The answer is—yourself.

To truly have a *Nothing Can Stop You year*, you need to overcome ingrained patterns that have been instilled by years of conditioning by parents, one's culture, and the media.

If you want to be rich, you cannot be normal. - Noah St. John

First, we need to identify what holds many of us back. We need to step away from the normal level of human awareness. We need to rise to a higher level. In a previous book I described something I call the Einstein Factor Secret. It's based on the Albert Einstein's comment: "You cannot solve a problem on the level in which it was created."

This following quote provides insight:

Nonresistance, nonjudgment, and nonattachment are the three aspects of true freedom and enlightened living. - Eckhart Tolle

Media and culture emphasize the opposite with messages like, "Resist, fight—that's the way to be a hero." "Judge everyone as less than ideal. Judge yourself as less than ideal." "Buy this and finally your life will be complete."*

Stop! In this section we will take a break from standard patterns of thinking. We'll explore new ways to move forward.

For example, inappropriate attachment can slow you down. We will discuss the benefits of using nonresistance, nonjudgment, and nonattachment in our interactions with others. And we will focus on being unstoppable.

Let's begin with nonresistance, since resistance can stop a harmonious interaction right from the beginning.

* A commercial perspective infuses much of media and culture. The advertising that forms the core of this influence centers on the premise that one needs to buy something to improve an implied deficiency in oneself or one's condition.

** I first shared material about nonjudgment, nonresistance and nonattachment in my book Nothing Can Stop You This Year!

* * * * * *

Nonresistance

I once learned a particular aikido move that required me to parry an oncoming punch with nonresistance, which is different from how I was trained. I had come from a background of using a traditional karate block when a punch was thrown at me during karate sparring. When forearm meets forearm, there is pain for both people. That is resistance.

Let's face it. Often, one does not win by using resistance. On the other hand, in aikido, one just guides the punch. You take the attacker in the direction that he or she was going. You don't stand in front–you sidestep. The force goes past you. That is nonresistance.

So, harvest the wisdom of aikido. Instead of being the rock standing against the raging water, be a canoe that flows with the water. We use the F.L.O.W. Process:

F – Focus on something bigger
L – Laugh it off
O – Open the possibility
W – Wonder

Focus on Something Bigger

Many individuals I have met get caught up in feeling small and vulnerable. This slows them down or stops them completely from expanding or improving their lives. What stops them?

The ego. Compared to your true self (or higher self), your ego is small. On the other hand, your true self is that part of you that is naturally courageous, brilliant, and connected with the goodness of the universe. The true self is expansive and bigger. Focus on it.

Shifting from the ego to the true self takes significant effort. Your ego is that part of you that is made up of fears, judgments, and feelings of being small and vulnerable. The good news is that when you shift from the ego to your true self, you step forward on a spiritual path that empowers you.

All religions, arts, and sciences are branches of the same tree.
- Albert Einstein

I could not say I believe. I know! I have had the experience of being gripped by something that is stronger than myself, something that people call God. - Carl Jung

So how can you have an experience of knowing? You need to get out of your own way. This is how workshops or retreats can be priceless. They can give you *an experience of knowing.*
Let me give you example. No, let me take you on a brief journey.
If you are in your home, go to your kitchen or bathroom sink. Now run the water. Make it pleasantly cool. Place your hand under the cool, comfortable water.
Do you feel it? Do you *know* it?
You see, writing about cool water is not the same as experiencing it.

We live our lives based on what we believe ... the
beliefs that precede our actions are the foundation
of all we cherish, dream, become, and accomplish ...
With few exceptions, our beliefs originate with what
science, history, religion, culture, and family tell us ...
The essence of our capabilities and limits may well be
based in what other people tell us. - Gregg Braden

Gregg's comment inspires me to choose beliefs that empower me to benevolently serve my readers and audience members. For example, I believe that this book will find people like you that I can serve. And I believe it will arrive in your hands at just the right time.

Also, I make sure to have experiences that empower me.

When you experience nonresistance, it is likely to be so unusual that it will surprise you. For example, one time I opened my mail and read something very troublesome for my business. But my response surprised me. Instead of feeling like throwing up and being overly concerned about a money-detail, I was ... wait for it ... calm.

What an extraordinary experience.

So, if someone asks me, "Can you be calm in the face of big trouble?" I can answer, "Yes. I know I can."

And when I was in that calm place, a thought occurred to me–*Money is replaceable when you're creative enough.*

How about that?!

Isn't that an empowered stance? Okay, I can grieve about the loss of money. But I can *simultaneously* do something to make things better! And, do you know what I get with that pattern? Hope!

True strength lies in submission which permits one to dedicate his life, through devotion, to something beyond himself. - Henry Miller

Henry's comment guides us in how to achieve a life filled with exuberance, fulfillment, and fun–get immersed in something.

One of my team members stated her difficulty with the word *submission*. She said that it is inappropriate to submit to a bully, for example. I responded that we're using the word submission in this way–Submit or give up your ego so that you can immerse in life. Devote yourself to something beyond yourself–a cause, Higher Power, your family, making life better for someone else.

Often I have felt the thrill of uniting with team members

to create something beneficial—a book or movie—for lots of people.

There is no coming to consciousness without pain. - Carl Jung

Carl's comment is an invitation to us to feel it all. Some of the greatest wisdom that I have gained in life has been part of a painful process. On the other hand, some people seek comfort first, and they seek to duck pain.

Instead, I'm inviting you to seek growth, opportunity, and fulfillment first. This has worked for me so many times. I attempt more things because I am interested in making a contribution and gaining spiritual growth. I have had enjoyable experiences that my parents could not even imagine. I've started and led companies, written books, traveled to various parts of the world, directed feature films, given speeches to top companies, and more. Such adventures involved trying new things and required me to deal with a significant amount of obstacles, disappointments, and sometimes fear. That price is worth it. I have become conscious of how I need to demonstrate courage and persistence in the face of obstacles.

Every year I do something new; some things work and some don't go as planned. Since I want things to be of high quality and benefit others, I find myself deeply concerned. I sometimes experience fear when things seem to take a bad turn. Then I had an idea that would help—This is Higher Power's book; I'm participating.

Can you imagine how much freedom and assurance I had when writing this book? I don't allow myself to be choked by writer's block because I trust that I'll be guided to clarity. Also, I work with trusted editors. I know writers who are choked by fear and thus do not complete books. My point is that faith can release anxiety, freeing one to take action, which may include utilizing the guidance of professional editors.

Focus on something bigger than yourself—Higher Power or a mission to make a contribution. When you do, your tendency to resist the process of exploring and enhancing your personal growth becomes smaller.

Principle:
When you focus on something bigger than yourself, your tendency to resist the process becomes smaller.

Power Questions:
How can you remind yourself to focus on something bigger?

How can you let go of your ego in favor of devotion to Higher Power or a cause?

Laugh It Off

I realize that humor isn't for everyone. It's only for people who want to have fun, enjoy life, and feel alive.
Anne Wilson Schaef

When I say, "laugh it off," I'm referring to a process of "shaking it off." Feel the pain, grieve when necessary, and find opportunities to experience laughter each day. Similarly, author Joel Osteen often says, "When someone has done you wrong, you need to shake it off." He invites his audiences to move on, focus on the blessings they already have, and move to a place of positive expectations.

A colleague said, "Isn't asking people to 'shake it off' a

callous comment? Like saying, 'suck it up?'" I responded, "This is the reason that I emphasize, "Feel the pain, grieve when necessary, and find opportunities to experience laughter each day." I acknowledge that life is tough. And I also know that brief laughter can give me the renewal to persist through hardship."

*Whenever you have truth it must be given with love,
or the message and the messenger will be rejected.
Mahatma Gandhi*

Finding a few moments to laugh each day may seem impossible when confronted with a truly painful situation. I have discovered that it is often the best, and sometimes the only way, to find comfort. For example, during the time that I wrote this book, I was a passenger in a car that was smashed in the rear by another car. The collision sounded like an explosion. Being a film director, I have heard special effects explosions on my sets. But the sound of impact between the two cars was scary.

Worse yet was how my head whipped backward. I didn't know my head could do that and that I could live through it. The pain was intense.

While I was in the hospital for six hours with a neck brace, I found myself calm and sharing humor with the X-ray and CT scan technicians.

At one point, a technician moved my head to place an x-ray plate below my neck. It made my neck hurt!

She said, "How's that?"

I replied, "I wouldn't recommend it."

She laughed, and I chuckled, too.

The point here is to not resist the moment. I just accepted the process I was going through. And I sought to make it as pleasant as possible to all involved.

We remember to avoid building up resistance in ourselves.

Nonresistance may be unappealing to some goal-oriented people. They may have the behavior pattern of resisting or raging against the obstacles that come up. Some people tell me that they must resist in order to accomplish their goals.

I find goals helpful. I prefer to persist and avoid loosing energy to the reflex of resisting. You see, I also trust that Higher Power will guide me to make the right decisions at the right time. Good decisions are part of the goal-achieving process.

For example, my company holds this mission:

We create encouraging, energizing edu-tainment for our good and humankind's rise.

How we reach these goals is up to Higher Power's guidance and our own plans and flexibility.

When a vendor sends back a proof (preproduction sample copy) of one of my books that looks terrible, I aim to flow with the process. I look for ways to enjoy humor throughout the day, and I avoid letting one disappointment bring me down.

Humor can be a salve as you still move forward toward what you want.

Principle:
Laugh often and well.

Power Questions:
How can you experience laughter everyday? Will you record a funny TV show, see a DVD, or call a friend who is fun to talk with?

Open the Possibility

When we listen first and hear someone out, we create a situation of harmony. - Tom Marcoux

Listening first to the other person opens the possibility that you will learn how to make a situation benefit both of you. Resistance can shut us down to connecting with someone. It can also keep us from entertaining a new idea. Often I have heard relatives say, "No, that won't work." And they're right. It won't work for them because they won't work it. Their comment says they are closed to a new possibility.

There were no rules for my father Robert Rossellini. It was life. I thought he brought my mother (Ingrid Bergman) so much optimism, so much vitality, and a sense of adventure. - Isabella Rossellini

I had been working extended hours when I heard this, and it inspired me to plan some fun times with my sweetheart.

The idea is to be open to the possibility of expressing your spontaneity and connecting with people who are important to you. So, I planned a short vacation in which she and I had joyful times with friends.

I was given courage. I was given a sense of adventure and that has carried me along. With a sense of humor and a little bit of common sense, it has been a rich life. - Ingrid Bergman

Ingrid's comment was made to reporters who were trying to get her to say how she regretted some of her decisions. Instead, she expressed her feelings about being open to possibilities. Ingrid didn't resist opportunities.

Is There an Appropriate Time to Resist Something?

Yes. In business we find that we must hold firm so that things work out in a fair way. For example, on three occasions I had to stand firm when family members had difficulties with certain merchants. They would get into some trouble and ask me to fix things. One time I had to say to a hotel manager, "That is not acceptable."

I create opportunities for nonresistance. In a conflict, I often use the power of language. I ask questions like, "How about we get this done with X or Y?" In this way, I guide the other person by showing my willingness to be flexible. My flexibility started a positive shift; and this inspired the hotel manager to demonstrate some flexibility, too.

So, in business, temporarily resisting includes some flexibility and an openness to new possibilities.

To shift your thoughts to new possibilities, you can use these methods mentioned by my clients:
- I take a deep breath and stretch. I feel better then.
- I say a prayer and ask God for guidance.
- I get up and walk to the water cooler and get a cup of water. By the time I get back, I have new ideas of how to move forward.

When we shift our thoughts and open ourselves to new

possibilities, we move beyond the limits of resistance. We step forward into the bright and fulfilling future that awaits our transformation.

Principle:
Find ways to pause, let go of resisting, and open the situation to new possibilities.

Power Questions:
How can you pause and shift your thoughts to new possibilities? Pick a problem that you're currently working on.

Write in your personal journal your answers to the following questions:
- What am I really concerned about here?
- How can I drop resistance?
- How can I be flexible?
- Can I offer a this-or-that solution? (Can I say, "How about we do X or Y?")

Wonder

To wonder invites freedom. It invites you to learn something new. You may even let go of a pattern that had previously imprisoned you.

For example, many people resist change in their relationships.

They think they know exactly what the other person will say or do. This leaves all the wonder out of the present moment.

Also, to think that you have figured someone out places you in a false superior position. This is the essence of judgment that we'll discuss in the next section.

Arguments are caused by two people racing to occupy the

victim position in the relationship ... Criticizing and blaming are like being in a hypnotic trance. - Gay Hendricks

Gay's comment invites us to substitute wonder for the habits of arguing, defaulting to a victim-position, and falling into the trance of criticizing and blaming.

Our true freedom is expressed when we open our awareness to new possibilities. It all begins with I wonder. Here are examples:
- I wonder how we'll avoid an argument this time and really listen to each other.
- I wonder what I'm really upset about, or if I'm just criticizing my spouse over something trivial.

Some people seem to be quickly and habitually labeling many things as "bad." Here is another view:

All the adversity I've had in my life, all my troubles and obstacles, have strengthened me ... You may not realize it when it happens, but a kick in the teeth may be the best thing in the world for you. - Walt Disney

Many of the extraordinary things that Walt Disney and his team accomplished were done when they wondered how to solve various problems.

It's kind of fun to do the impossible. - Walt Disney

To wonder is to gain access to a source of strength. You can wonder what your current problem or situation is preparing you for. Some of my clients hold the belief that Higher Power trains them for their later great accomplishments.

Great [people] are they who see that the spiritual is stronger than any material force, that thoughts rule the world. - Ralph Waldo Emerson

We can ask these questions in our own thoughts—I wonder how this helps me grow as a spiritual being. How does this strengthen me?

Principle:
Start with "I wonder about ..." and you open yourself to the freedom to discover new and empowering facets of life.

Power Questions:
How can you shift your thoughts so that you connect with the present moment and discover something to wonder about?

What is a problem that you're concerned about? Who can you talk with about the details you wonder about? Perhaps you'll say,

"I wonder where I can get advice about this. I wonder who can help me with this. I wonder if I'll find a solution in the morning if I get some rest and more sleep."

* * * * * *

Nonjudgment

We should not pretend to understand the world only by the intellect. The judgment of the intellect is only part of the truth.
- Carl Jung

Adopting an excessively critical perspective is a habit that can deny you much enjoyment and fulfillment in life. It is like a door that slams shut automatically. As Carl's comment implies, many of us may believe that our intellect holds all the answers. This denies us the power of intuition. Also, a number of people feel that human beings can access Higher Power's guidance.

The most beautiful thing we can experience is the mysterious. It is the source of all true art and all science. He to whom this emotion is a stranger, who can no longer pause to wonder and stand rapt in awe, is as good as dead: his eyes are closed. - Albert Einstein

We cannot get to the "mysterious," as Albert suggests, if we allow intellectualism to shut down our feelings, intuition, and empowering thoughts.

A Life Affirming Difference
I have repeatedly heard friends and audience members say things like, "Judgment is important. That's how I learn from the past, so I won't make the same mistakes again."

On the surface, this makes sense. And, yet, for those of us who want to experience more times of fulfillment, inner peace, and expanded success, there is an alternative.

To foster the optimal mindset, I recommend substituting the word discernment for judgment.* To be a "discerning person" implies flexibility, acceptance, and calmness. To be a judgmental person implies rigidness, defensiveness, and superiority.**

Discernment is a softer process that still allows for recognizing that a past behavior did not give you what you wanted so you can choose to act differently in the future.

* *The English language is a living entity. At the moment, a number of authors are writing about discernment and judgment, advocating for the adoption of a distinction between the two terms, along the lines advocated here.*

** *To further support the idea of using the two words differently (discernment and judgment), consider commentary on how the word judgment can function ambiguously. Rick Porritt observes that two different Greek words were originally used in the Bible, but translated into English as one—judgment. He discusses an occasion in Luke where the Greek word contains the idea of "condemning" (which is therein frowned upon). On the other hand, on an occasion in Corinthians the Greek word means "scrutinizing" (which is therein approved of). To Judge or Not to Judge?: Judgementalism & Discernment, Rick Porritt.*

* * *

On the other hand, judgment as personified in judgmentalism includes the dominating acts of the courts, who use judgments as instruments of force to silence opposing viewpoints. Whatever value this has to litigation, this process can cause havoc in our spiritual lives.

So right now, consider adopting the process and attitudes of discernment.

Because, once one acts like a judge, pronouncing one truth, one becomes blind to alternative viewpoints. For example, I had two clients, Matt and Kaya, a couple in the throes of a devastating argument. As an impartial third party, I could see that they were both right in a way. But they had already rendered their judgments about one another. Their rigid judgmentalism threatened their relationship.

Instead, they could have discerned what was working or not.

They could have recognized that they were both good people with different perceptions and priorities. That would have been a good foundation for resolving their differences.

Therefore, I invite you to adopt the flexible stance. Though it's easier to default to judgmentalism, discernment is more enriching, bringing us access to all the viable viewpoints. We avoid elevating ourselves to a superior position.

Your task is not to seek for love, but merely to seek and find all the barriers within yourself that you have built against it. - Rumi

Indeed, some of my friends have said that, during moments of arrogance, the universe took them down a peg or two. For example, one speaker I know was being abrupt with people because, she said, she was "so busy and in demand." Then one of her best clients suddenly dropped her services. She learned that bringing kindness to people is as important as bringing intellectual solutions.

To practice nonjudgment, we use the B.E.—H.E.R.E. Process:

B – Breathe
E – Enter with a benefit
H – Help
E – Energize
R – Respond
E – Engage

Breathe

When I dare to be powerful, to use my strength in the service of my vision, then it becomes less and less important whether I am afraid. - Audre Lorde

Judgment can be a reflexive response to what we're afraid of. At various times in my life, I have used deep breathing techniques to deal with fear and discomfort. Deep breathing has helped me feel strong. For example, I once had to negotiate with some people who acted in a mean and uncooperative manner. To put it simply, I felt at a disadvantage and I was angry and afraid of losing. Deep breathing helped me to calm down. Cool water helped, too. I made sure to take some time to be out of the room and away from the opposition.

With deep breathing and calming down, I had the ability to step away from making instant judgments. It helped me realize that my opponents were also afraid of losing. When I returned to the room, I was able to propose a solution that demonstrated my flexibility. My movement off my own position invited my opponents to alter their position a bit. We were then able to complete the transaction in a way that both sides saved face and gained something valuable.

For years, as an instructor of Comparative Religion to college students, I have noticed how a number of spiritual paths emphasize breathing, prayer, and movement. When I teach deep breathing at a spiritual bookstore, I often guide the audience through the Breathe in God Process. I ask, "Do you feel vulnerable or small? Would you like to feel connected to the goodness of the universe? Would you like to feel B.I.G. – that is, the Breathe in God Process."

Breathe In God
Step 1: Breathe in and allow your belly to inflate while simultaneously saying in your mind: "God"
Step 2: Hold your breath for one second.
Step 3: Breathe out while saying in your mind: "Thank you."

During my workshops, I have the audience include movements from tai chi and yoga as they breathe in "God." If you're interested, a number of DVDs related to tai chi and yoga are available at your local store or via the Internet.

*If the only prayer you ever say in your entire
life is thank you, it will be enough. - Meister Eckhart*

Principle:
Breathe deeply and calm down in order to quiet judgments and open the door to new possibilities.

Power Questions:
Think of a time when you were in an uncomfortable situation.

Can you imagine how first doing some deep breathing would have helped you slow down, calm down, and gather your thoughts? Imagine your next challenging situation— How can you step away, do some deep breathing, and then return with new energy?

Enter With a Benefit

When you make a judgment about something or someone, what do you really want? Do want to help the situation? Do you want everyone involved to feel better or gain something of value?

Enter with a benefit. That is, shift your thoughts from merely standing up for your rights to ensuring benefit for all involved.

The problem with judgment is that it puts you into a false superior position, like saying, "That's no good." But the difficulty with this approach is that we often discover later that our perception was off. And even if you keep your judgment as a silent thought in your mind, people can still feel it. They can pick up the subtle cues in your face and body language. One of my team members said, "Judging can be like a mirror. When I judge, I get impacted by other people's negative judgments." It's similar to when we hear that someone doesn't like us; we can have the tendency to dislike that person in return.

The meeting of two personalities is like the contact of two chemical substances: if there is any reaction, both are transformed. - Carl Jung

Sometimes, judgments seem perfectly rational, and we have judgmental thoughts by reflex. One time a friend was, in effect, hiding from the truth. My mind jumped to this thought:

People who live with their head in the sand get kicked in the butt. - Tom Marcoux

In the moment, making this comment might help someone, or merely get the person angry. Again, a judgment sounds like the speaker is putting him or herself above another. That does not inspire connection.

So how do we do this nonjudgment thing?
First, take a moment, breathe deeply, and ask yourself—Is there any chance I could be off about this thing? Am I perceiving this in a way that I may be missing something?

What jumps into my mind is a time when my perception was significantly off. I was 17 years old when my first love relationship ended, and I felt horrible. Later, I learned something troublesome about my former lover. I looked skyward and said, "Thanks for saving me from that one!"

To enter with a benefit requires that we have space to take in what is going on in this moment.

When we feel trapped, we can scratch at someone like a cornered animal. To feel trapped or upset usually involves some form of judging. We feel that someone is doing something that is unfair to us. In fact, we need to feel some form of freedom. We need freedom from our own pain that is expressed as judgments.

So where is your true freedom?

Would you join me in this present moment with the idea that we may not clearly perceive where our true freedom is?

The shoe that fits one person pinches another;
there is no recipe for living that suits all cases.
- Carl Jung

A number of spiritual paths invite us to approach life with humility. And it may surprise you that humility actually gives people an experience of true freedom.

I coined a phrase *healthy humility*, which includes having an appropriate sense of our place in the universe. We are beings connected with others. We have worth and value, and a human perception that can be limited in the moment.

The moment my attitude of cheerful humility
slips into self-righteousness or arrogance, the
universe will just as cheerfully step in with an
unexpected way to make me humble again.
- Gay Hendricks

Judgment is not a humble stance toward life. In striving for humility, seek to open your awareness. Look for ways in which a challenging situation can benefit everyone involved. Silently ask yourself, "How may I serve here? How can I take action so that everyone, including me, feels better and receives value?" Carry a notebook and quickly jot down the ideas that arise. You'll be glad that you did.

Principle:
Open your awareness and discover ways to benefit others.

Power Questions:
How can you shift the direction of your thoughts? Can you silently say, "He's a human being. How can I help him feel that he will win and do well in this situation?"

Help

It is time for parents to teach young people early on that in diversity there is beauty and there is strength.
- Maya Angelou

How can you quickly feel secure and connected with the goodness of the universe? Help someone. First, we need to acknowledge the value of diversity, and that our perception in the moment can be off. We really do not know what is best for another person. People are different in their preferences and their true needs. That person may need to go through some tough times to learn lessons for future situations.

Although we may want to help someone, that person may resist. When this happens, he or she is forging a personal path.

For this reason, I often ask, "How can I be supportive of what you're doing?"

Success is achieved by developing our strengths, not by eliminating our weaknesses.* - Marilyn vos Savant

Imagine how much good will you can inspire in someone when you are supportive and help the person experience her strengths.

With audiences, I mention that I'm a recovering Mr. Fix-it.

So, now I ask, "How can I be supportive of what you're doing?"

Principle:
Honor the fact that each person is on a different path. Ask, "How can I be supportive of what you're doing?"

Power Questions:
Remember a time when someone close to you was angry or emotional in some way. Did you react inappropriately? Did you pause and offer support? Are you a person with a spiritual focus who likes to say a silent prayer before an interaction? If so, consider this simple prayer, "How may I help?" If a spiritual path is not of interest to you, consider envisioning positive outcomes before you interact with the other person.

---

* This quote is about the value of finding one's best talents and devoting energy there. But it overstates the point. For example, one of my clients is best served in hiring a great illustrator instead of improving his meager cartooning skills. Otherwise, some weaknesses can be career-crippling. So careful self evaluation is critical in balancing attention between skills and weaknesses and deciding which to address.

Energize

Judgment hurts us because it often drains our energy. As soon as I have a negative judgment, I can feel my eyebrows scrunch up in tension. Instead, I'd rather flow in each present moment.

I Don't Want to Play That

I recently talked with a relative who started complaining. My spontaneous response (in my mind) was, "I don't want to play that." This came up because I had been doing some research on entrainment.

Entrainment is when we sync up with a rhythm. I know that when I feel tired, I can play certain songs that will lead me to perk up and resonate to their beat. I feel energized!

So when I thought, "I don't want to play that", I was thinking that I didn't want to play a "complaining song." Another way to look at it is, "I don't want to play that beat (or game)."

To avoid going into a downward spiral with my relative, I asked, "Oh, would you like to hear something on the radio?"

We were traveling in a car. A cheerful song lifted the mood. We have all witnessed the downward spiral of someone in a bad mood. For example, I remember a time in high school when a football player was in a bad mood and started a fight with me.

He continued to get in trouble with his teachers that day.

The solution is to pre-plan your responses so that you can, almost by reflex, do something healthy to lift your mood.

Choose, ahead of a tough time, what you would like to entrain to. My clients choose to take a brief walk, get a drink of water, listen to uplifting music, or play with a family pet. It's up to us to choose what we entrain to.

I avoid watching televised news broadcasts before I go to sleep. This guards my dreams from being disturbed and turned into nightmares. I prefer restful and renewing sleep. Some researchers state that nighttime television viewing adversely affects one's pineal gland.* We note that the pineal gland produces melatonin, a hormone that affects the modulation of wake/sleep patterns.

To energize is to make good choices about sleep, nutrition, exercise, and avoiding "downers." I have found that certain cartoon strips that emphasize complaining sap my energy.

It took repeated requests for me to get an old friend to stop sending me certain cartoons via email. Without exposure to those cartoon strips, my energy is protected and enhanced. I invite you to take similar action to avoid the downers in your life.

This book is about your nothing can stop you year. Enhance your energy so you have the ability to press on through obstacles.

Principle:
Pay attention and choose empowering energy to focus on.

---

* "Melatonin is a natural hormone that your body uses to regulate sleep cycles. Melatonin is triggered by exposure to light. The natural rhythms of the day are regulated by the pineal gland in what is called Circadian rhythms. ... at least one hour before sleep, turn off the television, dim the lights, and prevent exposure to bright lights. This will begin the trigger to your pineal gland that night is setting in. Lights with less of the blue color are also helpful, as they do not suppress melatonin." Melanie Grimes, adjunct faculty member, Bastyr University.

Power Questions:
What are the forms of downers in your life? Do certain activities, people, TV shows or other forms of media bring down your energy? How can you avoid the downers that are both inside and outside of yourself? How can you enhance your own energy?

Respond

Someone cuts you off in traffic. Do you respond or react?

Many of us will silently answer, "I react with anger. I mean, someone could have been killed!"

Judgment often happens when we take a spit-second jump into the past—into our past feelings, our past theories, and our past thoughts. We can jump to a belief like, "People who cut off others in traffic are ignorant [insert angry word here] who should have their licenses taken away!"

Here's something interesting—I started feeling irritable when I typed the above words. This is the problem with judgments–they raise our negative or irritable feelings to the surface.

Judgments are connected to beliefs.

Beliefs are often about the past. We believe things follow a pattern. We can make determinations about something based on our perception of what happened before. As I mentioned earlier, our perception in the moment can be off track.

Some people talk about how they cannot get a break. The truth is the past does not determine the future. You can make a new decision today that will alter the course you are on. It's as simple as the course correction that a pilot makes on the way to Hawaii. So, to enjoy life, we want to learn to respond in a positive way and not merely to react to something.

In my book, *Your Secret Charisma*, I wrote about how I restrained myself from reacting to my father after he cut off communication with me. I could have reacted negatively and expressed my pain with letters that attempted to "straighten him out." That just would have added fuel to the fire.

Instead, I chose to respond positively and found a different way to connect with my father. I sent him a happy-looking card that depicted Kermit the Frog playing the banjo.

> I wrote:
> Dad,
> Happy today. Thank you for holding me to high standards. This has made my life better.
> Love, Tom

My heartfelt comment helped my father feel better. Soon we were again talking on the phone and meeting in person.

Have the courage to act instead of react.
- Oliver Wendell Holmes

If I had followed suit with my father's unfortunate example, the situation could have turned into a grudge or a feud. When someone feels badly, delays in communication can lead them to become thoroughly entrenched in their own opinions and points of view. It becomes even more painful to loosen up and become less rigid.

Consider this old spiritual phrase, "Would you rather be right or happy?"

Apparently, when we look around at this world, numerous individuals prefer to be right—to the point of war and other horrible outcomes.

From this moment forward, let's choose to find ways to respond rather than to react to uncomfortable situations.

How Can You Respond Instead of React?
It's as easy as 1-2-3:
1. Breathe
2. Observe
3. Shift

Breathe
Breathing deeply is the first step to calming down so that you do not react immediately. You can say a prayer in your mind, like, "Higher Power, please help me calm down now."

Observe
Researchers note that people who meditate daily develop the ability to connect with their Observer.* The Observer is that part of you that can calmly look at your ego getting upset and say, silently, "Oh, there I go again."

When would it help you to flow to the Observer? Anytime you feel upset. My clients have mentioned frustrating times while driving, waiting in a long line, being placed on hold, or when a colleague rants on and on. At these times, the Observer can focus on calming behaviors like deep breathing, taking a walk, or drinking some cool water.

* "Harvard Medical School instructor Sara Lazar [discovered] people who meditate 40 minutes a day have 5 percent thicker brain tissue in the parts of the prefrontal cortex that … handle emotion regulation, attention, and working memory, all of which help control stress." Amanda Ripley, *The Unthinkable: Who Survives When Disaster Strikes–and Why*.

Shift

To shift, use a physical movement. For example, I sit down when I feel agitated. I recall having a heated conversation with my sweetheart. I sat down on the stairs.

As she started to move away from me, I shifted to a lower stair. In this way, I descended, following her to the garage.

Fear grows in darkness; if you think there's a bogeyman around, turn on the light. - Dorothy Thompson

Judgment can be a form of darkness. We have only our own perceptions to go with. We need to make space for the light of new ideas. As you can see, I enjoy quotations. The great writers and thinkers inspire me to see the world anew.

Principle:
Practice pausing before responding. When you do, you will avoid the loss of energy and time from inappropriate reactions.

Power Question:
How can you pause in order to give you the time you need to consider how to respond positively?

Engage

Many of us feel bad more often than we would care to admit. I have certainly gone through tough patches in my life.

Upon reflection, I realize that my focus had at times been in a downward direction. The key to avoiding this is to actually write down your repetitive negative thought patterns. Have you noticed yourself thinking things like, "I could lose my job if I don't get this right." "My spouse just doesn't care anymore." "No one understands the stress and pressure that I am under."

Sometimes negative statements like these can have a tinge of truth, and it may be necessary to consult a counselor or coach to make improvements. However, the important distinction is to identify what you can do and what you truly cannot control.

Know when you are caught up in an obsessive and destructive cycle of brooding with the same repetitive thought patterns.

To engage with this present moment, we need to release ourselves from brooding. Because I wanted to feel better and get more done, I learned to effectively change my focus by carefully choosing the questions I ask myself.

Let me show you the difference between a destructive question and a good question.

Destructive questions: Why does this always happen to me? Why can't I get what I want?

Good questions: What am I learning here? How can I do better next time?

The answer is in the question. Ask better questions.

How does this help me grow as a spiritual being?
- Tom Marcoux

To engage with life in a healthy and productive way — Choose your empowering questions.

I had been pursuing the idea of empowering questions for at least 12 years, and I wrote about them in seven books.

Then, just this year, I came across a book by Noah St. John

entitled, *The Secret Code of Success*. In this book, Noah describes what he calls "afformations," which he says are better than affirmations. Noah writes, "We are really forming new thought patterns, which form a new life for us."

Here are a few of Noah's afformations:
- Why am I so happy?
- Why do I have enough?
- Why am I so loved?
- Why am I rich?

What I like about afformations is that the process leads my mind to immediately reply with answers that start with "because." Here are a few of my personal "because" responses to Noah's questions:
- Because I have someone to love, something to do and something to hope for.
- Because I study everyday, I'm finding new ways to help people, resulting in increased income for my company.
- Because I actively live by practicing the virtues of healthy humility, generosity, compassion, and kindness.
- Because I'm surrounded by friends and team members who improve the projects that I begin.
- Because I'm doing things to help people improve their lives, and Higher Power guides me.

When I was earning my degree in psychology, I came across the book by Irvin Yalom entitled *Existential Psychotherapy*. Irvin wrote that the solution for human dilemmas is engagement. We engage or immerse ourselves in life as it is now. We fully devote ourselves to that which is positive and creates connection with other people and even Higher Power.

As I'm writing this, I'm listening to the song "Green

Light" sung by John Legend (with Andre 300). The lyrics talk about being ready to go right now. That's in line with engagement. We need to release our distractions and pain so that we can meet each moment with positive energy.

People focused on judgment often do not meet people in this moment right now. They see through a filter of prejudice and beliefs. Instead, let's aim to engage with each person and each moment in this instant. To engage creates connection and puts people at ease.

This is a process. Begin now so you can have a nothing-can stop-you year.

Principle:
Engage and immerse yourself in this moment now.

Power Question:
How can you release distractions and shift your attention to this present moment?

* * * * * *

Nonattachment

Nonattachment can often feel difficult or impossible to accomplish. When I talk with college students in my Comparative Religion class, nonattachment is a topic that feels strange to many in the room. Certainly, if we're talking about our friends and family, we feel truly attached. But imagine if we had the flexibility or even the softness to not be rigid about what we expect or demand from our loved ones. Unfortunately, it may seem natural to fall back to the pattern of—If you really loved me, you would never raise your voice or slam the door.

Nonattachment is the process of connecting with life as it is now, and rejoicing for anything that is positive. For some people, this may be a whole different view of nonattachment. They state that their view of nonattachment is being forced to let go of what they want or it's a process of not getting involved.

Instead, we can use nonattachment in a way that gives us more positive feelings. For example, one of my clients suffered an injury at work. It was then that she realized that she had a choice in each moment. She decided to live each day with fewer negative attachments. And she decided not to wait to be happy until after she recovered, which would take two months. She decided to appreciate any moment when her thoughts were not overwhelmed by her physical pain. For example, she soaked in a warm bath and relished the soothing feeling on her legs and torso.

Author Stephen Shapiro talked about "not looking for a specific outcome, but instead [you] are open to any outcome that could be of interest." In this way, one is nonattached to only one outcome. This is a process of backing off from demands in favor of having preferences. This is a softer, more flexible, and freer way to live.

In order to fully embrace the experience of nonattachment, we use the L.E.T.—G.O. Process:

L – Listen
E – Embrace the moment
T – Target Global Metaphors
G – Give
O – Observe

Listen

One way to loosen the grip of judgments and attachments is to listen first. Tell yourself, "Listen a moment." We need to notice that there is tension when two people meet; each person wants to express him or herself first.

When you listen first, you're winning. You're creating harmony and closeness as opposed to space and separation.

True listening is a constant reapplying of our attention back to the speaker. When you find that your mind drifts into judgment, you need to refocus on the speaker. Ask a gentle question. Here are examples:
- That sounds frustrating. What did you do next?
- How did you feel when that happened?
- What would you like to do now?

Never apologize for showing feeling. When you do so, you apologize for the truth. - Benjamin Disraeli

Although Benjamin may be pointing to a useful idea, I also realize that it's sometimes best to practice restraint and avoid expressing negative emotions in response to a speaker's thoughts. I have found it helpful to pause and listen to the other person first. After the other person has expressed herself, she will likely be open to hearing my viewpoint. And by then, I will likely have calmed down to a helpful degree.

Benjamin's comment also reminds me to listen to myself.

You are not upset for the reason you think that you are.
- Dr. Wayne Dyer

Wayne is referring to a spiritual concept that has been echoed throughout the centuries. The way to uncover what you're really upset about is to pay attention to your random thoughts and feelings. Capture them in a personal journal, and the process can reveal new insights. You may find yourself saying, "Oh! That's how I really feel about this. Then maybe I should switch gears now and do things differently."

As I mentioned elsewhere in this book, the ego is that part of us that is made of fear and feels small and vulnerable. The secret is to listen to your self. When you do, your ego will not cause havoc. When the ego is heard, it quiets down. That gives you space for nonattachment.

Here's an important distinction—I'm talking about hearing the ego and not necessarily obeying the ego.

The only way to tell the truth is to speak with kindness.

Only the words of a loving [person] can be heard.
- Henry David Thoreau

Being heard is crucial. Your ego wants to be heard. Be kind to your ego by listening to it. Then you can make plans and take action to nurture yourself or get nurturing from people you trust. Practice hearing yourself. I wrote a whole book on the topic, entitled *Be Heard and Be Trusted*, and in it I provide exercises that help you support yourself and to support others.

I want to emphasize that you need to be trustworthy to yourself. When you take care of your own needs, you'll find that you have the surplus energy you need to listen to other people first. And that's the first step to nonattachment. Listen first and avoid making immediate demands. You will then step forward in harmony.

Principle:
Listen first. Pause and make space for a new viewpoint.

Power Questions:
How can you pause and listen? Can you take a time-out and go to your car? Can you take a walk to the water cooler or around the block? Can you ensure that you have the energy to listen? Do you need more sleep, some recreation, or regular exercise?

Embrace the Moment

How can you embrace the moment?

First, you cannot do it if you're holding up your hands (metaphorically) and saying, "Oh, no! Take it away! Take it away!"

Here's a place to start—Find something to appreciate now –this second.

In this moment, say, "I am grateful for ..."

At this moment I am grateful for the opportunity to write.

Earlier today I finished grading my graduate students' final projects. Whew! I'm free! Free to do what? Free to write these words!

I'm grateful that you're reading these words. Being helpful to you is part of how I experience fulfillment in my life.

Now it's your turn. Embrace this moment. Let go (remember the L.E.T.—G.O. Process) of clinging to past judgments and expectations. Open your awareness to what is working right now.

Principle:
Embrace the moment by focusing on what you're grateful for right now.

Power Questions:
How can you remember what you're grateful for? Will you ask yourself, silently, "What am I grateful for?" Will you write your thoughts of gratitude in your personal journal? How could focusing on what you're grateful for increase your energy to have a nothing-can-stop-you year?

Target Global Metaphors

Some years ago when I was directing films, I held this metaphor—In a relationship, each person is like a bottle of water in a desert. Each person's good will is finite. Do you realize how scary this is? The bottle implies that the water is limited, and a desert without water is a deadly place.

In recent years I have sought to replace that water bottle metaphor with something more hopeful and healthy.

Now I focus on *Renewable Streams in the Forest*. This new global metaphor guides me to empowering questions like:
- How can I help people around me renew themselves?
- How can I renew myself?
- How can I create an environment that is nurturing?

A forest provides more natural resources, like streams, trees, and opportunities for food.

Now I ask you: How do you make sure that your relationships are like Renewable Streams in a Forest? Jot down any helpful ideas that occur to you in your personal journal.

I've learned to make sure that team members have time

and energy to renew themselves. For example, one of my team members is working on his own book. I make sure that he has a number of days off so that he can concentrate on his project.

He can then return to working on my projects with fresh and renewed energy.

> *I have treated many hundreds of patients. Among those in the second half of life—that is to say, over 35—there has not been one whose problem in the last resort was not that of finding a religious outlook on life. - Carl Jung*

Jung's comment is pointing us in an important direction. Now, imagine that I'm whispering to you. Sometimes that's how we hear a secret. How can you truly experience a nothing-can-stop you year? The answer—Find your spiritual path.

I have friends who are not interested in spirituality, and I appreciate their diversity. But I notice that they hold to their own moral compass. So, in essence, they have a guiding philosophy that supports them in their life's journey. Your global metaphors form a crucial element of your philosophy or spirituality.

Steve Jobs' following comment implies what's at stake.

> *Your time is limited, so don't waste it living someone else's life. Don't be trapped by dogma—which is living with the results of other people's thinking. Don't let the noise of others' opinions drown out your own inner voice. And most important, have the courage to follow your heart and intuition. They somehow already know what you truly want to become. Everything else is secondary. - Steve Jobs*

The idea is to not be overly attached to the approval of others.

I invite my graduate students involved with artistic pursuits to set aside some time each week to work on their own personal projects. In this way, regardless of what they will eventually do to earn money, they will find artistic freedom and satisfaction along their life's journey.

Go where your heart leads you. For example, one of my friends is now closing a deal to do a particular project. One year ago she had no idea that doing her own personal project would give her the necessary experience to be a candidate for a paying position. Intuition and Higher Power can guide you through the quiet voice of your heart.

For every beauty there is an eye somewhere to see it.
For every truth there is an ear somewhere to hear it.
For every love there is a heart somewhere to receive it.
- Ivan Panin

One [person] with courage makes a majority.
- Andrew Jackson

Now it's your turn. A global metaphor is a story you tell yourself that has been encapsulated in a brief phrase. What are your global metaphors?

Do you say to yourself, "It's too late for me." Or, "I'm still breathing. Better things are in store for me."

Write down your global metaphors in your personal journal.

Then identify any disempowering metaphors and write a turnaround metaphor next to it.

Here are examples:
- I'm too old (heavy, whatever) —> turnaround —> I can

use whatever I have at the moment to create what I want
- Life is tough* —> turnaround —> Life is vigorous and I'm up for it!

Take this moment. Yes!—this moment—to write for a mere 20 seconds about a global metaphor you hold that may be holding you back. Then write a turnaround metaphor. Consider posting it in many places so you will see if often.

Remember, a global metaphor is a story you tell yourself that has been encapsulated in a brief phrase. Tell yourself an empowering story. Choose your global metaphors wisely because they guide your habits, and habits lead to a destiny.

Principle:
Transform any global metaphor that does not empower you.

Power Questions:
How can you transform your disempowering global metaphors? Have you written a turnaround metaphor next to each disempowering metaphor? Will you use Post-It notes on your bathroom mirror and in your day planner to remind you of your new turnaround metaphors?

* The comment "life is tough" may be more accurately described as a meme. However for the sake of this discussion, I am including memes when I talk about global metaphors. My reasoning is that the position "life is tough" is a global position and it raises certain implications. Some people look on life being tough as a challenge. Others look on it as being completely unfair.

The idea of life being an "unfair game" would be viewed more as a global metaphor.)

Give

Nonattachment can be challenging when we feel that we've put a lot of effort into being good to someone. We feel entitled to being treated fairly in return. The tough thing is that a person in pain can flail about and say mean and unfair things. At that point, we're called upon to lend more than our fair share of patience. By the way, I want to make it clear that if someone is being abusive toward you—*get away from that person!* If you need help, do not hesitate to ask for it from a friend or a professional.

Many find it challenging to live harmoniously with family members. It helps to seek to become stronger personally so that we avoid returning negativity with more negativity. For example, if a family member is rude, perhaps we can demonstrate compassion by not yelling back. In this way, we avoid a negative downward spiral.

A number of authors talk about how relationships are where we go to give, and not just get. Sometimes we think we know what's best for someone else. Humility calls for us to remember that our perception of others may not be accurate. Knowing this, I choose to ask others, "How can I be supportive of what you're doing?"

> *Remember to be gentle with yourself and others ...*
> *Care for those around you. Look past your differences.*
> *Their dreams are no less than yours, their choices no*
> *more easily made. And give, give in any way you can,*
> *of whatever you possess. To give is to love. To withhold*
> *is to wither. Care less for your harvest than for how*
> *it is shared and your life will have meaning and your*
> *heart will have peace.*
> *- Kent Nerburn*

In the spirit of nonattachment, discover how you can improve your interactions. Step into the Observer part of your thoughts.

Ask questions like:
- What do I want here? Patience? I'll give it.
- A second chance? I'll give it.
- Some time to cool off? I'll give it.

Give us grace and strength to forbear and to persevere.
Give us courage and gaiety and the quiet mind.
- Robert Louis Stevenson

Robert's comment is a prayer to Higher Power. It reminds me that to give is divine.

Happiness is not a goal; it is a by-product.
- Eleanor Roosevelt

Earlier in this section we talked about engagement as the solution for human dilemmas. Engagement is immersing in life. When talking with clients and audience members, I often hear how people helped others, and then felt their own mood improve—as a by-product.

The basic rule of free enterprise: You must give in
order to get. - Scott Alexander

Business is ultimately a spiritual path. - Gay Hendricks

I have worked with thousands of people during the current economic crisis. Even in this challenging time, I have found that business owners find hope when they focus on how to give first, which starts a positive cycle with their customers.

When we give, we experience joy, and nonattachment flows naturally.

Principle:
Give first and start a positive cycle.

Power Questions:
Imagine that you want to achieve something that you have never done before. Relationships are crucial for new accomplishments. How can you be supportive in your relationships? How can you give? Would you like to ask, "How can I be supportive of what you're doing?"

Observe

All of man's troubles stem from his inability to sit quietly in a room alone. - Blaise Pascal

Some people see this quote and say, "What would a person do when sitting alone quietly?" The answer—Observe. Observe your thoughts and learn to step into the Observer—that part of you that is calm. Many people who meditate learn to observe their thoughts. The Observer doesn't get upset because the Observer is not identified with only a small part of you.

My background in martial arts has been helpful when I have acted in feature films. At my current age, I do not kick in the manner I did when I was 25 years old. This bothers me.

But it bothers me for only a moment because my Observer

kicks in and provides me with the space I need to switch the direction of my thoughts.

> Me: I don't kick like I did when I was 25 years old. I'm getting older. Things are slowing down.
> Observer: Oh, there I go again. Whoa! Stop! What can I be glad about?
> Me: I'm glad that I can still kick! And walk! And run! I'm glad that I still feel healthy. I'm glad that it's not all about kicking (a small part of my life). It's really about the journey that I'm on.

In the long run, perhaps it is helpful that we cannot rely on our youthful bodies to be our identities. Life's journey certainly invites us to practice nonattachment. As one of my editors said, "We trade higher kicks for higher wisdom."

The truth will set you free. But first, it will piss you off.
Gloria Steinem

So, are you feeling upset? Okay. Write about it for 20 seconds in your personal journal. Observe your angry feelings. Imagine how you are more than these particular feelings. You are more than your body, for example. You are a spirit having a human experience. See how you can practice nonattachment to your ego's obsessions.

Nonattachment Opens the Door to Happiness
How? Let's remember Eleanor Roosevelt's comment,: "Happiness is not a goal; it is a by-product."
Immerse yourself in life and happiness will show up as a pleasant visitor.

Happiness is not in the mere possession of money; it lies in the joy of achievement, in the thrill of creative effort. - Franklin D. Roosevelt

There is only one happiness in life, to love, and be loved. - George Sand
(pen name of Amandine Aurore Lucile Dupin)

How do we express love to someone in the moment? We listen!

We make a switch from judgment to nonattachment. At times, someone will say something and my fast-moving mind will have a quick retort. But I pause to do the loving thing. I listen and say, "Okay." When I say okay, I mean, "I hear you and you are valuable to me." Sure, I could say something clever, but that just gets me separation—the opposite of closeness.

What we call the secret of happiness is no more a secret than our willingness to choose life. - Leo Buscaglia

Observe your choices. Choose life. Choose to listen and to respond.

That is happiness; to be dissolved into something completely great. - Willa Cather

Give yourself opportunities to express your creativity. It takes creativity to do many things in life. You're creative when you can balance work, family, and other activities. You're creative when you nurture yourself and take care of your body through nutrition and exercise. You're creative when you try new activities and, perhaps, discover a new hobby.

> *Generosity is the antidote that balances our tendency to be greedy. Humility is the antidote that softens our arrogance. Vulnerability is the antidote to being overly guarded. Being of service balances our tendency to be self-absorbed. Honesty [integrity] is the antidote to our tendency toward deceit. Willingness is the antidote that softens our stubborn nature. Compassion is the antidote that balances our intolerance. The antidotes transcend our limited 'I' perspective, bringing us back into alignment with our higher selves and into the collective heart. - Debbie Ford*

Debbie's comments are some of the most profound and helpful ideas I have heard. I will now provide questions that can help you switch, in the present moment, toward a spiritual path using the virtues she describes.

1. Generosity—How can I be helpful in this situation?
2. Humility—How am I part of the equation of this problem? Can I be missing something here?
3. Vulnerability—Is this a situation in which I can admit my mistake and show how I'll do better next time?
4. Being of service—How can I be supportive of what you're doing?
5. Integrity—How can I support my feelings of being whole and act in a way that brings benefit to all involved?
6. Willingness—Am I'm being unnecessarily stubborn? Can I be willing to find a solution that benefits me and the other person? Can I be flexible in some way?
7. Compassion—How might the other person be hurting?

Can I help somehow? Can I ask, "What would be helpful to you?"

Practice these questions and memorize them so that when you're under stress, your default setting will ask empowering and responsive questions.

All happy people are grateful. Ungrateful people cannot be happy. We tend to think that being unhappy leads people to complain, but it's truer to say that complaining leads to people becoming unhappy.
- Dennis Prager

Pointing derisively to others and talking about what you don't want drops your energy and furrows your brow. Talk about the good and what you want. Don't give the bad equal time.
- Tom Marcoux

Some years ago, when I was learning about healthy ways of living, I described to a friend how someone I knew was living in an unhealthy way that caused him problems. But then I had an A-ha! Moment. Discussing something negative brought down my energy in that moment. And it was not doing my friend any favors either.

I usually avoid giving bad examples, and just emphasize the positive direction I'm aiming for.

Gain Energy to Consistently Focus on the Positive

When you feel a personal energy crisis, the solution is to devote at least six minutes each day to meditation or prayer.

Years ago I used to invite people to just grab a spare three minutes. Then I discovered that I needed three minutes just to calm down. Now I devote six minutes for meditation, even when I'm taking a train or plane to a speaking engagement.

I call these moments, the Six-Minute Makeover. I realize that makeover often refers to a change in appearance. But here we're talking about a true makeover—a deep transformation.

Researchers have noted that people who meditate regularly report bringing those moments of tranquility into their daily lives.* They smile more and feel more at ease.

To Express Courage, One Needs Energy
Remember that you can get a boost of energy from the Six-Minute Makeover.

One isn't necessarily born with courage, but one is born with potential. Without courage, we cannot practice any other virtue with consistency. We can't be kind, true, merciful, generous, or honest.
- Maya Angelou

Being deeply loved by someone gives you strength, while loving someone deeply gives you courage.
- Lao Tzu

---

* "Psychologists are increasingly seeing the benefits of meditation in easing disorders like depression and anxiety. The Centre for Mindfulness Research and Practice at Bangor University funds research into meditation.

'The research being done at Bangor is looking into the medical benefits of meditation, shorn from any religious beliefs or Buddhist philosophy,' says Martin Wilks, a chartered counseling psychologist who uses mindfulness practices with his clients," writes Esme McAvoy.

A number of my clients report that the Six-Minute Makeover gives them time with God, who strengthens them. Sounds great to me!

The size of your success is measured by the strength
of your desire; the size of your dream; and how you
handle disappointment along the way.
-Robert Kiyosaki

A daily spiritual practice of meditation or prayer gives you unconditional support. You don't feel alone. Higher Power waits for you to show up for your Six-Minute Makeover.

Strength does not come from winning. Your struggles
develop your strengths. When you go through
hardships and decide not to surrender, that is strength.
- Arnold Schwarzenegger

You will likely feel peace during your Six-Minute Makeover. You will have a brief vacation from problems. You will feel and know that what you are and what you have is enough—in the moment.

If you realize that you have enough, you are truly rich.
- Lao-tzu

Nonattachment opens the door to creating situations that improve on what you have experienced. After going through an ordeal, we often discover that things were not as hard as we had feared. Unfortunately, we had been attached to a false expectation. Instead, approach each new minute as something that has never before occurred.

For example, years ago, as a sole proprietor, I would always dread doing the paperwork for my taxes. But, when I added a pleasant component, I'd be surprised at how easy the process was. My strategy—energizing music certainly helped uplift my mood.

I now approach projects in the spirit, "This might flow easier than I expect. I'll just enter each new moment as it arrives."

It is love, not reason, that is stronger than death.
- Thomas Mann

Where does calm energy come from? Your *Six-Minute Makeover*.

I invite you to try an experiment. Pick a certain number of days to experience a daily session of six minutes for meditation, prayer, or quiet time.

An experiment is quiet and gentle. For example, I used the experiment method to see if I would add jogging to my daily life. I said to friends, "I'm going to do a 30-day experiment. I'm going to run for ten minutes each day to see how I like it."

Try a Six-Minute Makeover. After a number of sessions, you'll see a difference. It's worth it.

Principle:
Practice going to the place of the Observer. When you do, you'll be able to engage in nonresistance, nonjudgment, and nonattachment.

Power Questions:
How can you shift to the place of the Observer? Does deep breathing help you? Have you tried a Six-Minute

Makeover? Do you truly want a nothing-can-stop-you year? Are you willing to try something new? Can you reward yourself for your first efforts?

Conclusion to the Book Three

Now that we have viewed the processes of nonresistance, nonjudgment, and nonattachment, I have a question for you,

"What are the benefits of these three processes?"

The answer–saving time and saving energy. Imagine a conflict eases when you back off and do not attempt to force someone to comply with your request. Imagine that you have the energy to listen first. Then you can avoid the default setting of resistance.

When you resist another, you inspire that person's resistance.
- Tom Marcoux

What is often necessary is to curb our own resistance and shift to pausing and hearing out the other person first. Ask a gentle question like, "So how did it feel when ...?"

Meanwhile, judgment is one of the biggest forms of resistance.

We have covered the F.L.O.W. Process so that you can shift your thoughts and feelings.

The F.L.O.W. Process includes:

F – Focus on something bigger
L – Laugh it off
O – Open the possibility
W – Wonder

Finally, nonattachment is very helpful, but it takes practice.

It is hard to be tolerant of people who are intolerant of you.
- Marianne Williamson

Marianne's comment reminds me about the practice of nonattachment. For example, I have family members who find some of my actions strange. Even on a vacation day, my practice is to get up, write, and then exercise. I'll even write occasional notes when traveling. I have learned to be nonattached about whether certain family members show approval for my habits.

Now it's your turn. What in your life bothers you? Note details in your personal journal. Can you imagine how you might let go of demanding certain responses from people? How much more energy would you have if you were practicing nonattachment?

Earlier I shared John Gray's story about one of his clients, a woman lamenting the poor treatment and neglect she received at the hands of her mother. As her therapist, John Gray guided the woman to realize that she was fortunate to have a kind aunt who acted as her surrogate mother. Eventually, the woman was able to practice nonattachment with her mother's indifference, and she rejoiced in the loving aunt that she had.

So much energy is lost to frustration because we hold expectations about how we want things to go. For example, as my recent birthday approached, friends asked about my birthday plans. I had already decided to make a plan that included space for spontaneity. I said, "I'm going to let things unfold moment by moment."

My target is to feel it all—the joy, the disappointment, the love, and the hope.

Now it's your turn. How much more ease would your life include if you lived moment by moment? Consider the old refrain, "I learned how to predict certain rain; schedule an outdoor wedding."

To practice nonattachment, a person can schedule an outdoor wedding with a cheerful backup plan in case rain appears.

Author Mike Robbins has a valuable question:

What am I willing to do today to step out in life?
- Mike Robbins

Mike's comment reminds us to try new things everyday. I invite you to re-read this section on nonresistance, nonjudgment, and nonattachment to find actions that you can place into your day planner and experiment with.

[We] defuse stress by hearing our own feelings and
needs ... Empathy is emptying the mind and listening
with our whole being ... Staying with empathy, we
allow speakers to touch deeper levels of themselves.
- Marshall B. Rosenberg

Marshall's comments remind us to hear our own feelings and needs—and take action to support our own energy. We will then have the surplus energy to live with empathy in the moment. Otherwise, if we're stressed out, our minds will be full of worries. Such negative energy can foster an atmosphere of resistance.

I invite you to use the Six-Minute Makeover (meditation or prayer) to empty your mind and ego so that you can be present with others moment by moment. Remember to stay in empathy.

When you do, people will find it easier to explore their deeper personal levels with you. This is an enjoyable result that I have experienced over and over.

> *True success relies on the support and buy-in of others. You must understand the reasons why your vision is important, and you need to be able to clearly communicate that importance ... The expectations we exceed today become the seed for new opportunities in the future. - Tony Jeary*

True success can blossom when you practice the processes of nonresistance, nonjudgment, and nonattachment. This is something that "the happiest man in the world," Buddhist teacher Yongey Mingyur Rinpoche, knows. Yongey gained that label of happiest man when researchers used fMRI technology to scan his brain. They discovered that the happiness areas of his brain were exceptionally active.

Yongey knows that we need to practice, practice, practice.

Eventually, the processes will become part of you, and you will discover success and fulfillment at a higher level. Albert Einstein said, "You cannot solve a problem on the same level on which it was created." The good news is now you will be able to live on a higher level. This is an experience that will bless your life.

BOOK FOUR
THE WORKBOOK: "WHAT I LEARNED FROM REALLY SUCCESSFUL PEOPLE—THAT HAS MADE ALL THE DIFFERENCE"

Introduction:

Welcome! This workbook is unique. It is a compilation of my comments that arose from television, radio, Internet, and print interviews that I have given. It is a joy for me and my team to present this information to you—now all together in one place. I invite you to get the most from this workbook by writing down your answers in a personal journal or notebook. Even just devoting 20 seconds to write your answer will empower you.

Table of Contents:
Sections:
1. Build the Castle First
2. Your Personal Brand—The Safety Net in the New Economy
3. Add Fulfillment to Success

4. Find What is Better than Self-Discipline (Trigger-Sequence)
5. Release the Music that's Inside You
6. Create Maximum Productivity
7. Enhance Your Relationships
8. Make A Project Successful and Handle Problems Effectively
9. Nurture Yourself and Enjoy Life
10. Conclusion

Section One: Build the Castle First

Tom, you lead people to fulfill big dreams. What is a guiding principle of your leadership?

Tom: Walt Disney said, "Build the castle first." When Walt Disney was building Disneyland, he had the workers construct the castle first. Then all the workers knew what they were building—a place of magic and joy.

So when I start a motion picture project I go beyond the screenplay. I have versions of the poster created. I have music composed. I give people a preview of the feelings that the movie will inspire. This is my way of "building the castle first." This is how I get investors, actors, and production personnel all on the same page. For example, at this moment, my team is preparing a trilogy of science fiction motion pictures entitled *TimePulse*. To give the team clarity, we are also doing a graphic novel. The images of the graphic novel form the pre-production storyboards. You can view images at www.TimePulse.com

To build your castle first is to have a vision of what you want to achieve. How is your life going to improve once you get the job, complete a project, or improve a relationship? You need to gain clarity. You need a target. What has helped me for years is to focus on principles. For example, I remember the principle "build your castle first."

The second part is to identify your role models, and the third part is to answer the question: "Where is the joy?"

In response to these questions, my client, Marina wrote down this: "My business grows so that I have two subcontractors doing graphic designs. My role models are Gina R. and Emily Z. The joy is in a) playing with ideas, b) seeing the finished projects and c) seeing the smiling faces of happy clients."

The part about "where is the joy?" is very important. At one time, I found myself feeling fatigued and without energy for a project. I had to ask myself "where is the joy?" and that served to jumpstart my energy.

Write down what your vision is for any project or area of your life. Remember to "build the castle first."

Identify your role models.

Where is the joy?

* * * * * *

Section Two: Your Personal Brand—The Safety Net in the New Economy

So what can a person do?—now with all the layoffs, the outsourcing of American jobs to India and elsewhere—and the struggle to get enough clients to stay in business?

I emphasize that *the personal brand is the safety net for people in the new economy.*

What is a personal brand?

I remember what author Peter Montoya wrote: "A personal brand is a promise of performance that creates expectations in its audience. Done well, it clearly communicates the values, personality, and abilities of the person behind it." As a person with a powerful personal brand, Oprah Winfrey emphasizes values: "Though I'm grateful for the blessings of wealth, it hasn't changed who I am. My feet are still on the ground. I'm just wearing better shoes."

How is your personal brand a safety net?

The personal brand becomes the shortest distance between you and getting what you want. Want to protect your job? Use a personal brand. Want to get clients? Use a personal brand. Want to feel good about your work? Use a personal brand.

Why is a personal brand going to make you feel happy?

Your personal brand blossoms from your true self. Your true self is that part of you that feels strong, on purpose, and connected with what is good. For example, my client Mindy is a graphic design consultant. Her true self is an artist. She helps people communicate by using the best images. At this time, Mindy is working with me to develop her personal brand—something that emphasizes her expertise and heartfelt focus on helping people communicate powerfully. Mindy tells me that she now feels better about her business and what she does. I remember what Oprah Winfrey said, "Always continue the climb. It is possible for you to do whatever you choose, if you first get to know who you are and are willing to work with a power that is greater than ourselves to do it." That's why I emphasize the true self.

Also, the personal brand helps you communicate effectively with people.

I remember what C.J. Hayden, author of *Get Clients Now* wrote: "What you'll discover if you begin to meet clients in person, talk to them on the phone, and ask directly for their business, is that it gets easier the more you do it. It will build your confidence in yourself—and the confidence your prospective clients have in you—at the same time. If you're in the business of serving people, your best marketing tool is your own voice. So put it to work and start talking to them."

When people think of a brand, they think of Nike® or Mercedes. Not just a feeling. How does a personal brand fit into this?

We can think of a personal brand as a communication tool. For example, the *San Francisco Examiner* labeled me as "The Personal Branding Instructor." This conveys a quick idea. We need to realize that we now live in a "sound bite society." It has to be clear, in few words. My personal brand of "America's Communication Coach" clearly conveys how I help people. They can trust that I have expertise in communication skills. A brand is the shortest distance to trust.

Where does a personal brand start?

It starts inside you. With your true self. Answer these questions: a) What are four major ways you get satisfaction in your work? b) What are your key strengths? c) What are you best known for? (a question posed by Lois P. Frankel).

Here's an example of my answers:

a) My satisfaction comes from I like playing with ideas, and I enjoy helping clients in these three areas: Power Communication, Power Time Management and Branding (naming your product or business—or creating a personal brand).

b) One of my key strengths is my ability to find the emotional key for Power Communication, Power Time Management and Branding. This means that I help people inspire emotion and action in others.

c) I am best known for my enthusiasm, compassion and methods for encouraging people to take action to improve their lives.

What are the major ways you get satisfaction in your work?

What are your key strengths?

What are you best known for?

* * * * * *

Section Three: Add Fulfillment to Success

Is there an idea that you think about everyday?
Mother Teresa said, "Let no one come to you without leaving better." There's really a lot of joy when you focus on making a meaningful contribution. I encourage my students. For example, when I teach the three online courses that I wrote, I make sure that each email message I send encourages the student. In a similar direction, Marianne Williamson said, "Nothing liberates our greatness like the desire to help, the desire to serve."

Martin Luther King, Jr. said, "Everybody can be great... because anybody can serve. You don't have to have a college degree to serve. You don't have to make your subject and verb agree to serve. You only need a heart full of grace. A soul generated by love."

Focusing on how you can serve helps you add fulfillment to your success. I remember Steven Spielberg said, "I no longer have to prove anything to anyone. I no longer have to prove anything to myself. I just need to stay interested." This reminds me that as I help others and express my creativity—I can connect with my true self. My true self is that part of me that realizes that I am a human being and not just a "human doing." Focusing on being a human being (feeling connected and whole) is a constructive fixation. On the other hand, a destructive fixation would be making one's self-esteem solely dependent on external accolades—external praise.

Oprah Winfrey has a number of ideas about significance: "The key to realizing a dream is to focus not on success but on significance—and then even the small steps and little victories along your path will take on greater meaning. . . . For everyone of us that succeeds, it's because there's somebody there to show you the way out. The light doesn't always necessarily have to be in your family; for me it was teachers and school. . . . My philosophy is that not only are you responsible for your life, but doing the best at this moment puts you in the best place for the next moment. . . . You get in life what you have the courage to ask for."

Don't you have a favorite quote from Gandhi?

Yes. Gandhi said, "I am neither a man of letters nor of science, but I humbly claim to be a man of prayer." Before I speak before an audience or to a class of my students at the Academy of Art University, I hold this prayer in my mind, 'How may I serve?' What has helped me is to have a perspective about my place in the universe. At this time, I am writing a book, and to my friends I say, "It's Higher Power's book. I am participating."

To add significance to your success, write down two of your favorite spiritual or philosophical quotes.

How do you serve (or how can you serve) as you do your work?

* * * * * *

Section Four: Find What is Better than Self-Discipline (Trigger-Sequence)

What about discipline and creating the success a person wants?

Discipline is important. For example, Zig Ziglar said, "Discipline makes the difference. Exceptions are what destroy peoples' dreams and keep them from being significant." The idea is to make a commitment to yourself and keep it. If you decide to exercise twenty minutes a day, and you keep that commitment you get a double-reward: you gain the physical benefits and you feel great about yourself.

But wait a minute. Many people say self-discipline is hard. The good news is that it does NOT have to be so hard. The real power is in a well-prepared Trigger-Sequence.

What is a Trigger-Sequence?

It includes four things: a trigger, emotion, thoughts and behavior.

Here's a vivid example.

Someone I know "Stephen" suffered when his pet died.

The **trigger** was the death and the **emotion** of sadness.

Another emotion was the desire to escape the pain of sadness.

The automatic **thought** was comfort food as in reaching for an orange cupcake.

The **behavior** was eating not just one cupcake but three.

The solution is to set-up a Replacement-Behavior before one is confronted with a stressful situation.

Stephen decided to **replace** orange cupcakes with oranges.

Some people would say, "You just have to have discipline to avoid eating junk food." Instead, I emphasize that you want to prepare your Trigger-Sequence to work in your favor by pre-setting up your Replacement-Behavior.

Here's another example: I have used this process of a Replacement-Behavior. At night, I would replace reacting to the desire for food with getting a glass of water.

How does this Trigger-Sequence work better than discipline?

The idea is that you prepare your Trigger-Sequence to work naturally in your favor. Then, when the trigger shows up, you naturally go into a better place. You do not have to force yourself and practice onerous self-discipline. Bob Greene, the personal fitness trainer for Oprah Winfrey, points out that many people reach for food when they are really thirsty. When I shed 12 lbs. in 20 days, I drank five eight-ounce glasses of water a day. I prepared my Trigger-Sequence to avoid food when I really needed to be hydrated. This process really helped.

Identify a trigger, emotion, thought, and behavior you want to modify. How can you add a Replacement-Behavior into the mix?

* * * * * *

Section Five: Release the Music that's Inside You

Tom, you do so many things. You direct feature films, compose music, write books, give speeches, and teach college courses. Tell me about this.

Dr. Wayne Dyer said, "Do not die with your music still inside you." Over the years, I have found ways to express my creativity. I encourage everyone to start expressing their creativity on a small level and build their skills. For example, anyone who wants to be a filmmaker can borrow a video camcorder and start making a one-minute film next week. Dr. Wayne Dyer also said, "Some people live the same year 10 times." Each year, I do something different—something new—something challenging. I keep a list of these milestones achieved in my business plan binder. An interviewer once asked me to describe my life with a few words. These words came up: "adventure, educator, freedom, and creative."

How can you express your creativity on a small level?

What would be the next level up from the small level?

What would be your ideal ways (top level) of expressing your creativity?

* * * * * *

Section Six: Create Maximum Productivity

Do you ever find it hard to relax or slow down?
Sometimes. I remember what Mary Shelley said, "Nothing contributes so much to tranquilize the mind as a steady purpose—a point on which the soul may fix its intellectual eye." Yes, this is the same Mary Shelley who wrote *Frankenstein* when she was 19 years old. I also realize that the most effective person alternates periods of activity with recovery. So on weekends, I make sure that I stay away from the computer for a span of some hours.

Some people find it hard to make their new small business successful. They're concerned about their personal productivity. What do you suggest?
I remember what author Jay Conrad Levinson wrote: "No matter what you think you do for a living, you're really in four businesses at once. The first is. . .the one mentioned on your business card. The second is the marketing business…. The third is the service business…the fourth is the people business…. There's a close correlation between your interest in people and your ability to convince and motivate them." What I do is help clients build on the principles noted in Jay's quote.

Many of my clients write down the four business areas on their weekly schedule and then write "next action" under each business area category. Here is the secret: when my clients write down the "next action," they start feeling better. Now they have something to focus on. They can schedule the next action for the next day or even for a month away. But they have found their bearings. There are multiple steps to improve your productivity:

1) Find your values.
2) Target your goals.
3) Write down your projects.
4) Note a "next action" next to each project.
5) Schedule the actions you can do in your day planner, personal digital assistant, etc.

Some people who own businesses find themselves approaching burnout. What can they do?

I remember that Michael Gerber wrote about how a small business really thrives when it is organized like a franchise. He said that the business is better when it is "a systems-dependent business—not a people-dependent business . . . The purpose of a system is to free you to do the things you want to do . . . The purpose for going into business is to get free of a job." So his idea is that the business owner establishes systems so that she or he doesn't have to be there in the store.

Now, the question is: how can you use these ideas to make your life better? Here's how: My client, Sandra wrote down how a prospective client first hears about her and every step Sandra (or her team member) needs to do to gain that person as a paying client. Now, when Sandra receives a query-email, she or her assistant just opens the binder and goes down the list of actions. This saves time. No time is lost to pausing, hesitating or re-thinking steps.

Pause and take note about how you can set up a system for your business (if you have one). For example, a number of authors and personal coaches, write and post a blog article each week. This is a process of gaining an audience and using one's blog effectively to build one's credibility.

Do you have a productivity secret when it comes to making a product?

Yes. When naming the product, put the benefit into the title like *Online Secrets to Build Your Brand* or *Power Time Management: More Time, Less Stress and Zero Procrastination.*

Write down the steps for gaining a client/customer (if you're in sales or own your own business). How can you make this into a system?

* * * * * *

Section Seven: Enhance Your Relationships

When it comes to supporting your romantic relationship, do you have a guideline?

Dr. Gay Hendricks wrote: "To improve your relationship: a) accept feelings, b) keep agreements, c) turn complaints into action or a request and d) tell the truth." My sweetheart and I focus on these elements, and we have enjoyed happy years together. The idea of turning complaints into action or a request is as simple as making a choice between a) buy a separate tube of toothpaste or b) ask, "Would you please squeeze the toothpaste tube at the bottom?" I suggest buying a separate tube of toothpaste.

What can you tell us about building stronger friendships?

Thomas Chandler said, "To love a person is to learn the song that's in their heart, and to sing it to them when they have forgotten." Sometimes, I tell a friend this quote and then ask him or her: "So what is your song?" Recently, I called a friend and encouraged him to consider the advice of a wise mother who said, "Do what makes you happy." She didn't say, "Do what is easy." Instead, she invited her daughter to make the efforts to build a better life.

What agreements do you need to pay more attention to? What can you do to support your agreements better?

Which friends/family members do you want to talk with about "To love a person is to learn the song that's in their heart, and to sing it to them when they have forgotten"?

* * * * * *

Section Eight: Make A Project Successful and Handle Problems Effectively

To make a project turn out successfully, do you have a process?

Albert Einstein said, "Imagination is more important than knowledge." I start by imagining good outcomes and phenomenal outcomes. I remember an old phrase: "Success is met expectations." So I identify who are the stakeholders—that is, who will benefit from the project. Then I find out their expectations. I seek out the stakeholders and ask them questions. I find that using my imagination and then gaining knowledge to fulfill my targets is helpful.

If my project is about making my own business profitable, what will help me?

I remember what Brian Koslow wrote:

"The most profitable businesses are not necessarily those with the most skilled employees or the best products. They are the ones with the best marketing strategy and the best leadership."

I guide my clients to write down in their weekly schedule "next action" items under the headings of "best marketing strategy" and "best leadership."

For example, in today's business world, good leadership includes building credibility through an effective use of one's website or blog. When it comes to a website or blog, a good leader has a vision. Such a vision includes a clear image of one's ideal client/customer and what unique advantages the client would gain by using your services/products.

In essence, a leader provides the vision and then guides team members to fulfill that vision.

When dealing with problems, what are your first thoughts?

I remember the phrase: "Problems are landmarks of progress." Then I remember, Albert Einstein's comment: "You cannot solve a problem on the same level on which it was created." I talk with someone I trust, and I identify what I am afraid of—that might happen. Then I figure out ways to avoid bad outcomes. I figure out ways to turn the situation around. The companies that I buy from repeatedly are the ones who corrected any problems with courtesy and care. A problem—like a late shipment—can be turned into a chance to really demonstrate how much you want to make amends. This creates a new level of commitment in the customer. The customer has seen how you improve a tough situation, and then the person's trust in your company goes up.

What can you do related to "best marketing strategy"? Which books or other resources can help you?

What can you do related to "best leadership"? Which books or other resources can help you?

* * * * * *

Section Nine: Nurture Yourself and Enjoy Life

I often feel overwhelmed. What can I do to nurture myself and find "my smile" again?

I'm glad that you mentioned this topic. My audiences tell me that they like my strategies centered on the acrostic "SAY YES." Here are details that I reveal when I speak on the topic: *Say Yes to Yourself: Secrets to Overcome Stress and Change in Your Workplace.*

S – step off the stage
A – accept better care
Y – yield to recovery
Y – yearn for energy
E – encourage your best
S – support your team

1. Step off the stage

It takes a lot of energy to keep up your "professional face." It's a façade. You need times during your workday when you can catch your breath, and step away from other people. Just a little time will do. Years ago, I worked for a particular organization in downtown San Francisco. There was no spare room at this firm. During my lunch break, I would step onto the balcony with a chair, sit down and meditate. You can rest in a restroom stall. You can go to your car and rest there. You can rest by walking on the steps between floors. Here is a question to ask yourself:

How can I step off the stage?

2. Accept better care

Many of us get so caught up in our work that we do not take care of ourselves. Imagine, if you saw your best friend working in the manner you do, would you counsel him or her to take an appropriate break? It is likely that you would. Here is the important question to ask yourself, repeatedly through the workday:

How can I take better care of myself right now?

3. Yield to recovery

I use the word "yield" with care. When we drive a car, we must yield to oncoming traffic. And in life, we must yield to the truth that researchers have discovered about optimal human functioning: humans do best when they use an Activity-Recovery Pattern. This means the person is active and then rests. This is shown by top tennis pros. In a two-hour match, they are active for 20 minutes. They rest in between outbursts of energy. For an office worker, the person can write a report in the morning, then later "rest" by doing something less taxing ... perhaps, doing some photocopying.

How can you use the Activity-Recovery Pattern?

4. Yearn for energy

I discovered this one day when I was feeling unusually fatigued. I had work to do, and normally I would have felt a great connection. I knew that writing this particular report would ultimately help people. The problem was, at that moment, I did not feel the connection. Then I asked myself, "Where is the joy?" I then realized the joy was when I would be speaking before an audience and sharing these ideas. That would be when I would have fun. That was where the joy was. At that point, I had a connection to the purpose for the report, and I felt energetic.

Where is the joy?

5. Encourage your best

Many people hold great fear about their jobs. The solution is to become known at your workplace for being excellent in the skills highly valued in that workplace. Ask yourself, "What I am best known for?" Then, make sure that you do what will help you be known as a crucial team member.

What are you best known for?

6. Support your team

In order to experience support from your co-workers and supervisor, you need to support those individuals. They are all true individuals with different personality styles. This next set of insights is built on the discoveries of a number of researchers. Personality styles can be viewed in this manner:

a) *The Lion:* A director-type person who is a hard-charger with little patience. This person wants to hear the brief details and to know the impact on the bottom line.

b) *The Dog:* A relater-type person who values a human connection over changing to make things better. This person likes routine.

c) *The Beaver:* An analytic-type person who is a detail-obsessed, engineer-type person. Often, this person is slow to make a decision.

d) *The Peacock:* A socializer-type person who loves talking about ideas with people, and who is quick at decision-making but poor on follow-up.

Here's an example. When Theresa was presenting to a group of people, she took into account their personality styles. She reached the "accountant type" (or Beaver-type) audience members by using an acrostic like P.R.E.S.E.N.T. These audience members appreciated the methodical approach. She appealed to the "Relater type" (or Dog-type) audience members by asking, "What are you hoping or expecting that I will be talking about today?" Then, she wrote down their topics/questions. Then Theresa said, "We will get to as many of these details during our time together—as we can." Finally, Theresa appealed to the "Director" (or Lion-type) audience members, by checking off the topics/questions as she went through them. The director-type person appreciates the progress shown by checking off the topics.

Here is another example. John has a "director" (Lion) style, and he compensates for it. In the middle of a conversation with Susan, a relater (Dog), John slows down and asks gentle questions. He listens first. On the other hand, when working with Sam, an analyzer (Beaver), John invites Sam to prepare in a special way before their next weekly meeting. John says, "Sam, write some notes on three alternative solutions. Then endorse one and tell me your reasoning when we meet on Friday." In this manner, John supports Sam's analytic personality style. John also supports his own "director" personality style that calls for brevity.

For clarity, here are the four personality styles: director (hard-charging, brief, bottom-line oriented), relater (listener, dislikes change), analyzer (likes graphs/tables, slow to make a decision) and socializer (decides quickly, verbal, poor on follow-up).

How can focusing on personality styles help me do better?

* * * * * *

Conclusion

Here is a list of the quotes mentioned in this workbook section. I invite you to print them out and place them in your wallet or purse for instant inspiration. Inspiration is really about setting yourself up with positive Trigger-Sequences (see Section Four). And glancing at these quotes may prove helpful.

1. "Build the castle first." – Walt Disney
2. "Let no one come to you without leaving better."
– Mother Teresa
3. "Nothing liberates our greatness like the desire to help, the desire to serve." – Marianne Williamson
4. "I am neither a man of letters nor of science, but I humbly claim to be a man of prayer." – Gandhi
5. "Do not die with your music still inside you."
– Dr. Wayne Dyer
6. "I no longer have to prove anything to anyone. I no longer have to prove anything to myself. I just need to stay interested." – Steven Spielberg
7. "Though I'm grateful for the blessings of wealth, it hasn't changed who I am. My feet are still on the ground. I'm just wearing better shoes." – Oprah Winfrey
8. "Some people live the same year 10 times."
– Dr. Wayne Dyer
9. "Nothing contributes so much to tranquilize the mind

as a steady purpose—a point on which the soul may fix its intellectual eye." – Mary Shelley

10. "Our fears must never hold us back from pursuing our hopes." – John F. Kennedy

11. "The key to realizing a dream is to focus not on success but on significance—and then even the small steps and little victories along your path with take on greater meaning. . . . For everyone of us that succeeds, it's because there's somebody there to show you the way out. The light doesn't always necessarily have to be in your family; for me it was teachers and school. . . . My philosophy is that not only are you responsible for your life, but doing the best at this moment puts you in the best place for the next moment. . . . You get in life what you have the courage to ask for."
– Oprah Winfrey

12. "To improve your relationship: a) accept feelings, b) keep agreements, c) turn complaints into action or a request and d) tell the truth." – Dr. Gay Hendricks

13. "Imagination is more important than knowledge."
– Albert Einstein

14. "You cannot solve a problem on the same level on which it was created." – Albert Einstein

15. "Discipline makes the difference. Exceptions are what destroy peoples' dreams and keep them from being significant." – Zig Ziglar

16. "Nothing is free. If we don't pay for it with money, we pay for it with our time, energy or health." – Carmen Renee Berry

17. "What are you best known for?" – Lois P. Frankel

18. "[A business functions better when it is] a systems-dependent business—not a people-dependent business . . . The purpose of a system is to free you to do the things you want to do . . . The purpose for going into business is to get

free of a job." – Michael Gerber

19. "The most profitable businesses are not necessarily those with the most skilled employees or the best products. They are the ones with the best marketing strategy and the best leadership." – Brian Koslow

20. "A personal brand is a promise of performance that creates expectations in its audience. Done well, it clearly communicates the values, personality, and abilities of the person behind it." – Peter Montoya

21. "What you'll discover if you begin to meet clients in person, talk to them on the phone, and ask directly for their business, is that it gets easier the more you do it. It will build your confidence in yourself—and the confidence your prospective clients have in you—at the same time. If you're in the business of serving people, your best marketing tool is your own voice. So put it to work and start talking to them." – C.J. Hayden

22. "Always continue the climb. It is possible for you to do whatever you choose, if you first get to know who you are and are willing to work with a power that is greater than ourselves to do it." – Oprah Winfrey

23. "No matter what you think you do for a living, you're really in four businesses at once. The first is . . .the one mentioned on your business card. The second is the marketing business…. The third is the service business…the fourth is the people business…. There's a close correlation between your interest in people and your ability to convince and motivate them." – Jay Conrad Levinson

24. "To love a person is to learn the song that's in their heart, and to sing it to them when they have forgotten."
– Thomas Chandler

The best to you.

A FINAL WORD AND
THE SPRINGBOARD TO YOUR DREAMS

Congratulations on your efforts with this book. Realize you can truly increase the flow of financial abundance in your life and experience spiritual joy. Imagine that you're connected with all that is good in the universe. Now, some of us might say, "I'm looking for love."
Imagine a shift to "I *am* love."

Love is the real work of your life. — Robert Holden

The decision to be the presence of love is the most powerful influence you can have in any situation in your life and in this world. — Robert Holden

Imagine that whatever you're doing it is a possibility to express love and kindness.
In this final section, I will now share methods for you to feel powerful and improve your productivity. We'll use the W.O.W. process:

W – watch out for work-addictions
O – oppose time-wasters
W – wake up to joy

1. Watch out for work-addictions

Pause for a moment. Ask yourself: **"Am I doing the top priority that serves my (our) highest good?"**

(I mention "our" because many of us are motivated by doing good things that benefit others.)

Many of us get caught up in what I call a "hobby" or "work-addiction." For example, Joe simply likes working with Photoshop. He's a business owner (and leader), and he has a top priority to lead his company's next marketing campaign. Instead, he tinkers with Photoshop. Not good.

It would help if Joe would call Photoshop his "hobby" and then schedule time with Photoshop as recreation.

At work, however, he can turn over Photoshop projects to one of his team members, or he could hire a contractor. And then Joe can focus on his top priorities for his business.

If Joe persists in tinkering with Photoshop when he's called to do high priority work, he will remain in a work-addiction.

We are called to be truthful with ourselves. Be sure to ask yourself: Am I doing the top priority that serves my highest good?

2. Oppose time-wasters

Ask the question: **"Does this strengthen me?"**

If it doesn't strengthen you, it's wasting your time.

I invite you to realize that you need to take good care of yourself so that you can make good decisions. Sometimes a decision must be made quickly and you must take fast action.

I recommend that you look at your daily activities. Ask this about each activity: Does this strengthen me?

For example, someone may gather with people who tease him mercilessly. Instead, he can be truthful in his own thoughts. He can ask, "Does this strengthen me?" and he can seek to develop a different circle of friends.

Be conscious to drop that which does not strengthen you.

3. Wake up to joy

Recently, one of my clients complained that she had lost enthusiasm for her own business.

I invited her to take a look at her life and, in particular, the tasks required by her business. I asked her this question: **"Where is the joy?"**

When you find the answer to where is the joy, you can "work backwards." For example, years ago, I felt myself slow down on a report I was writing. Then I asked myself: "Where is the joy?" And I realized that the joy was in presenting the material for an upcoming speech. So I visualized communicating the vital information to an audience.

I found that my personal energy increased. And I efficiently completed the report.

Ask yourself: **"Where is the joy?"** — and discover what energizes you.

* * *

I remember the *3 Vital Questions* (noted above) with this mnemonic device "PJS" (you could pronounce it pj's):
1. Priority
2. Joy
3. Strength

And the questions are:
1. Am I doing the top **priority** for my (our) highest good?
2. Where is the **joy**?
3. Does this **strengthen** me?

This is part of a process I call *Time Leverage,* which is better than some methods of traditional time management.

Why? You're focused on increasing your personal energy and effectiveness.

That's a big benefit that may have more power than a standard time management skill of using lists.

Focus on your priorities, develop energy from having joy in your day, and be sure to do things that strengthen you.

* * *

As we come to the close of this book, I'm grateful to have had the opportunity to share insights with you.

To gain more value from this book, be sure to go through it and develop your own To Do List. Take some action. Any action towards improving skills and promoting yourself is helpful. I often say, "Better than zero."

Please consider gaining special training through my coaching (phone and in-person), workshops, presentations and Top Five Group Elite Video Training.

As you continue to work toward expanding your financial abundance, you are likely to come up against some tough situations. To be supportive I've written a number of books . . .

- Darkest Secrets of Charisma
- Darkest Secrets of Persuasion and Seduction Masters: How to Protect Yourself and Turn the Power to Good

- Darkest Secrets of Negotiation Masters
- Darkest Secrets of Making a Pitch to the Film and Television Industry
- Darkest Secrets of Film Directing
- Darkest Secrets of the Film and Television Industry Every Actor Should Know
- Darkest Secrets of Spiritual Seduction Masters
- Secrets of Awesome Dinner Guests: What Walt Disney, Steve Jobs, Oprah Winfrey, Albert Einstein, Martin Luther King, Jr., Helen Keller, and John Lasseter Can Teach You About Success and Fulfillment
- Success Secrets of Rich, Smart and Powerful People: How You Can Use Leverage for Business Success

See my blog at
www.BeHeardandBeTrusted.com

The best to you and may you continue to change the world,
Tom
Tom Marcoux,
America's Communication Coach
Motion Picture Director, Actor, Producer, Screenwriter
P.S. See **Free Chapters** of Tom Marcoux's 19 books at http://amzn.to/ZiCTRj

Titles include:
Be Heard and Be Trusted
Nothing Can Stop You This Year
Truth No One Will Tell You
10 Seconds to Wealth
Your Secret Charisma
Wake Up Your Spirit to Prosperity

The Cat Advantage
— and more.
(For coaching, reach Tom Marcoux
at tomsupercoach@gmail.com)

EXCERPT FROM
BE HEARD AND BE TRUSTED:
HOW YOU CAN USE SECRETS OF THE GREATEST COMMUNICATORS TO GET WHAT YOU WANT

2nd Edition by Tom Marcoux,
America's Communication Coach

Table of Contents

How You Can Radiate Charisma
* Guest Article by Dr. Tony Alessandra
How Billionaires & Millionaires Use C. O. M. P. E. L.
Handle Fear & Mistakes with Skill
* Guest Article by Dr. Fred Luskin
Reduce Risk
* Guest Article by Dr. Elayne Savage
Power Thought / Physiology Process
Solution-for-Error Plan
How to Help People Feel at Ease
Overcome the #1 Obstacle to Happiness
Truth No One Will Tell You
Great Communicators Win with Job Interviews
* Guest Article by Mike Robbins
Win When Dealmaking and Negotiating

Be Heard and Be Trusted on the Telephone
How to Use Your Personal Brand as Your Shortcut to Trust
Great Communicators Make Good Luck
* Guest Article by Marc Allen
* Guest Article by Linda and Charlie Bloom
Great Communicators Give Compelling Speeches
* Guest Article by Jay Conrad Levinson
Great Communicators Persuade with Ease
Secrets about Networking and the Media
* Guest Article by Guy Kawasaki
A Final Word and Springboard to Your Dreams
Special Offer for Readers of this book .
Excerpt from Darkest Secrets of Persuasion and Seduction Masters
by Tom Marcoux
About the Author

* * * * * *

Part I, Section 1
How You Can Radiate Charisma
and Get What You Want

What terrific things could be in your life if you were charismatic?

Imagine if you could easily gain people's agreement and cooperation. Top professionals come across as charismatic. *The American Heritage Dictionary* defines "charisma" as "personal magnetism or charm."

A charismatic person makes each of us feel like the most important person in the room. How is this done? The charismatic person listens to others and connects with their pain.

A charismatic person often uses an effective story to engage people's emotions and open listeners to benevolent influence.

A charismatic person expresses compelling messages. Dictionary.com defines "compelling" as "to force or drive, especially to a course of action … to overpower … to have a powerful and irresistible effect, influence." We want to overpower inertia, low moods, and procrastination. We want to take action consistently to create the best possible situations in our own lives.

An interviewer said to me, "I'm not comfortable with the idea of 'force.'"

"All right, let's focus on having a good intention first," I replied. "Instead of force, let's aim to 'move' a person's emotions. "For example, when I was ten years old, my piano teacher knew how to persuade me to practice. She helped me see how much I improved when I practiced. She moved my emotions so that I could feel and enjoy the benefits I was getting. She also cleverly had me practice a song that I really wanted to play."

In essence, my piano teacher was a compelling communicator. She was heard and trusted by me. And that's what you'll learn how to do in this book.

How much would your life improve if you could easily get people to say yes to you? What if you could easily get them to want to say yes?

- "Yes! You're hired. The job is yours."
- "Yes! Here's your raise and promotion."
- "Yes! I'll marry you."

- "Yes! Here's $200,000 to develop your entrepreneurial idea."
- "Yes! I'll buy your product."

What if you could get what you really want—faster than you ever imagined?

That was both the opportunity and the problem for my client Sarah. She confessed, "I need to improve my communication skills."

"How would that give you what you really want?" I asked.

For a moment, she frowned in thought.

"And what do you really want?"

"A raise and a promotion!" she said with sudden clarity.

"What would that take?"

"My boss would have to trust me with higher profile assignments."

In essence, Sarah didn't just want to improve her communication skills; she wanted to be heard and be trusted.

With my guidance, Sarah learned to use the skills found in this book. She learned methods to increase her confidence, speak well to authority, and feel higher self-esteem.

For 26 years, I have helped thousands of clients and audience members become great communicators. In fact, an earlier version of this book was accepted as a textbook by Cogswell Polytechnical College and included in that college's time capsule.

The capsule is set to be opened in 2100. Even in 2100, the timeless principles of warm and trustworthy communication will be valuable.

In this book, we will cover story after story that highlight how many, including twelve billionaires and millionaires, communicate successfully to make things happen. You will also learn directly from the articles and comments of a number of other great communicators.

This book is filled with principles that can help you relate to people on a higher level of connection and cooperation.

As to methods there may be a million and then some, but principles are few. The man who grasps principles can successfully select his own methods. The man who tries methods, ignoring principles, is sure to have trouble. - Ralph Waldo Emerson

For compelling communication, you need to do two things:

1. Seize the attention
2. Create a connection

We want our communication to be not merely pleasant, but compelling. We want people to cooperate with us, to take action in the direction we're proposing. To help you make this year the best year of your life so far, we will explore the C.O.M.P.E.L. process.

C - Connect with the listener's pain
O - Open with genuineness
M - Maximize leverage
P - Pull with a story
E - Ease
L - Lift

"Be so good—they can't ignore you," said writer-actor-comedian Steve Martin in response to the question, "How do you gain big success?" With this book, you will become so good at influencing people. And, I will add, be so trustworthy that they want to do for you.

Let's move on. Let's learn how to be charismatic and influential ...

Connect with the Listener's Pain

Where does it hurt? Did your attention go to your body? Did you feel tension in your neck area?

To make your message compelling, you need to uncover your listener's pain.

Ask someone what he or she wants. The easiest way for the person to reply is to say, "What I don't want is to stay in this job.

Here's what I do not like in my current situation." The person talks about what causes pain.

What I have in my heart must come out; that is the reason I compose. - Ludwig van Beethoven

Beethoven reminds us that what is in our hearts must come out. Similarly, as great communicators we need to help our listener express his or her heartfelt pains and desires. By helping your listener identify "where it hurts," you can help her achieve a transformation.

The power of transformation reminds me of the journey of Gay Hendricks, the bestselling author of *Five Wishes* and cofounder of The Hendricks Institute. Years ago, when he was a 300-pound tobacco addict in a horrible marriage, he felt the need to reinvent himself. He says that what sustained him was a deep inner knowledge of where he was going—toward a life of soul awareness and creative fulfillment. Today he has a fit, 180-pound frame, over six feet tall. Gay was blocked. His blockage was made of conflicted feelings: he couldn't decide whether to continue studying in the University of New Hampshire counseling program or follow his desire to be a writer. Dwight Webb, an insightful professor of his, suggested, "Why not write about counseling?" Was there any reason Gay could not put his feelings and inner experiences into poems and articles connected with his profession? The answer was that he could do both things he loved. He could pursue psychological counseling and writing. Gay's poems were published in counseling journals and caught the eye of a professor at Stanford University, who helped Gay gain a fellowship to that institution for his doctorate. Gay went on to a 25-year academic career and wrote over 20 books.

When I contacted Gay a while ago, I discovered that he had found fulfillment as a screenwriter-filmmaker and as a seminar leader through The Hendricks Institute. Gay's journey shows that it is an "and" universe, not a "this or that" universe. The point is that Gay's professor Dwight Webb provided great coaching. He listened to Gay's pain and shared a new way to view the situation.

The only service a friend can really render is to keep up your courage by holding up to you a mirror in which you can see a noble image of yourself. - George Bernard Shaw

When you really want to be heard and be trusted, focus on something that will benefit the other person. Be the person's friend. Take the appropriate actions to help him or her.

With a number of my clients, we focus on the transition from novice salesperson to coach-to-action. As George

Bernard Shaw points out, you as the coach can hold a friendly mirror up to your listener, who will then be able to see a noble image of the self. This noble image can inspire the listener to agree to whatever you're offering. And as the coach, you can help the person enjoy more in life and work.

It is above all by the imagination that we achieve perception and compassion and hope. - Ursula LeGuin

First, connect with the listener's pain. Then, with the knowledge you have gained, you can focus on helping. You can help people imagine a better personal future.

People in general are starved for the experience of being heard. - Gordon Livingston, M.D.

Get what you want by giving people what they crave: to be heard.

Principle:
Connect with the listener's pain and show that you have the remedy.

Power Question:
How can you gently ask questions that allow you to identify the listener's pain?*

*NOTE: * To get the maximum benefit from this book, devote at least 20 seconds to writing down the answer to each Power Question in your personal journal.*

Open with Genuineness

When you are content to be simply yourself and don't compare or compete, everybody will respect you. - Lao-tzu

"We don't need you to be perfect; we need you to be genuine," I say to my graduate students who seek to be better public speakers and pitch-givers.

*Do what you said you were going to do,
when you said you were going to do it,
in exactly the way you said you were going to do it.
You won't ever get any better business advice than that.
Be there when you said you would be there.
Deliver when you said you would deliver.
Call when you said you would call.
Be a person who can be counted on
by keeping his word every time.
- Larry Winget*

Have you ever been afraid that when you are giving a speech, your mind might go blank or you might lose your place? The solution is, *be genuine.*

When I coach CEOs and company presidents in how to give speeches, I help them express genuineness. This helps the CEO connect with the audience and motivate team members.

End of Excerpt from
Be Heard and Be Trusted: How You Can Use Secrets of the Greatest Communicators to Get What You Want
Copyright 2012 Tom Marcoux Media, LLC

Purchase your copy of this book (paperback or ebook) at Amazon.com or BarnesandNoble.com

See **Free Chapters** of Tom Marcoux's 22 books at http://amzn.to/ZiCTRj

ABOUT THE AUTHOR

Tom Marcoux helps people like you fulfill big dreams. Known as America's Communication Coach, Tom has authored 22 books with sales in 15 countries. One of his *Darkest Secrets* books rose to #1 on Amazon.com Hot New Releases in Business Life (and in Business Communication). He guides clients and audiences (IBM, Sun Microsystems, etc.) to success in job interviewing, public speaking, media relations, and branding. A member of the National Speakers Association, he is a professional coach and guest expert on TV, radio, and print, and was dubbed "the Personal Branding Instructor" by the *San Francisco Examiner*. Tom addressed National Association of Broadcasters' Conference six years running. With a degree in psychology, Tom is a guest lecturer at **Stanford University**, DeAnza, & California State University, and teaches public speaking, science fiction cinema/literature and comparative religion at Academy of Art University. Winner of a special award at the **Emmys**, Tom wrote, directed, and produced a feature film that the distributor took to the **Cannes film market**, and the film gained international distribution. He is engaged in book/film projects *Crystal Pegasus* (children's) and *TimePulse* (science fiction). See TomSuperCoach.com and Tom's well-received blog at www.BeHeardandBeTrusted.com

Tom Marcoux can help you with **speech writing** and **coaching for your best performance.**
As Tom says, *Make Your Speech a Pleasant Beach.*
Join Tom's Linkedin.com group: *Executive Public Speaking and Communication Power.*
Get a **Free** report: "9 Deadly Mistakes to Avoid for Your Next Speech and 9 Surefire Methods" at

http://tomsupercoach.com/freereport9Mistakes4Speech.html

Tom Marcoux has trained CEOs, small business owners, and graduate students to speak with impact and gain audiences' tremendous approval and cooperation. *Learn how to present and get thunderous applause!*

"Tom, Thanks for your coaching and work with me on revising my speech at a major university. Working with you has been so enlightening for me. Through your gentle prodding and guidance I was able to write a speech that connects with the audience. I wish everyone could experience the transformation I have undergone. You have helped me discover the warm and compelling stories that now make my speech reach hearts and uplift minds. This was truly an empowering experience. I cannot thank you enough for your great assistance." — J.S.

Become a fan of Tom's graphic novels/feature films:

Science fiction: *TimePulse*
www.facebook.com/timepulsegraphicnovel

Fantasy Thriller: *Jack AngelSword*
type "JackAngelSword" at Facebook.com

Children's Fantasy: *Crystal Pegasus*
www.facebook.com/crystalpegasusandrose

See **Free Chapters** of Tom Marcoux's 22 books at http://amzn.to/ZiCTRj

Special Offer Just for Readers of this Book:

Contact Tom Marcoux at tomsupercoach@gmail.com for special discounts on books, coaching, workshops and presentations. Just mention your experience with this book.

www.ingramcontent.com/pod-product-compliance
Lightning Source LLC
Chambersburg PA
CBHW071311110426
42743CB00042B/1274